TODAY'S INSPIRED LATINA

Volume III

LIFE STORIES OF SUCCESS IN THE FACE OF ADVERSITY

JACKIE CAMACHO-RUIZ

1

Today's Inspired Latina

This book is a compilation of stories from numerous Latinas who have each contributed a chapter and is designed to provide inspiration to our readers.

It is sold with the understanding that the publisher and the individual authors are not engaged in the rendering of psychological, legal, accounting or other professional advice. The content and views in each chapter are the sole expression and opinion of its author and not necessarily the views of Fig Factor Media, LLC.

For more information, contact:

Jaqueline Camacho-Ruiz
Fig Factor Media, LLC | www.figfactormedia.com
JJR Marketing, Inc. | www.jjrmarketing.com

Cover Design & Layout by Juan Pablo Ruiz
Printed in the United States of America

ISBN: 978-0-9971605-1-2

To all the young Latinas with
big dreams and aspirations.

Contents:

Acknowledgements

My heart "beeps" with excitement as we publish Today's Inspired Latina Volume III. This magic would not be possible without the authors of Volume I and Volume II and their relentless commitment to inspire the community.

Collaboration is possible when a solid team comes together with the same vision, to elevate Latinas. My deep gratitude goes to our team that made this possible: Irene Anzola as the project manager, Karen Dix as our editor, Juan Pablo Ruiz as our creative director and designer and the countless of volunteers that made every event possible.

May the magic of this international movement continue to inspire many lives.

Introduction

JACQUELINE CAMACHO-RUIZ

It all started with a small inspiration. I was going to gather an impactful collection of inspiring stories from ten Latinas into a book and call it "Today's Inspired Latina." Before I knew it, 10 stories became 27, and Volume I was quickly followed by Volume II and now...Volume III.

I stand completely awed by the launch of Volume III because even in my wildest dreams I never imagined this possibility. Volume I, and then Volume II, become the catalyst for so much more. Authorship in the book has led so many Latinas to the confidence and support they needed to attain speaking engagements, secure media opportunities and even launch businesses. Best of all, I've witnessed how one single book fostered a vibrant, beautiful community of Latinas who are deeply connected in a special way as a "Today's Inspired Latina" author.

These ladies meet each other for the first time as friends already, knowing each other as "book sisters" and sharing an experience that for many has been life-changing. They are already connected in a positive way and ready to offer their friendship and connections to help their sister succeed. Every book sister understands that success is a shared venture, and by building each other up and helping others pave the way for success, we all win.

As I've watched these ladies, bathed in the warm glow of their new status as an author, I've noticed that the most driven and adventurous of the group have experienced the most growth. They have used their authorship to elevate the community and share their stories through events at libraries, schools, churches, and even over the airwaves and the internet. Those ladies understand that the book can be a stepping stone to something even greater and more fulfilling.

I do too. That's why I recognize that a movement like "Today's Inspired Latina" can only take shape through the efforts of many, infusing their magic, connecting and collaborating. For my part, I will remain committed to my life mission of creating vehicles of inspiration as long as the community is in need. Whether it be through more volumes in this series or projects through my mentorship nonprofit, The Fig Factor Foundation, I want to continue to do whatever I can to build supportive communities for those who have a dream and need help fulfilling it.

To all you past, present and future "book sisters", know that we are one heart. I encourage you to embrace your potential and live to your fullest as one of "Today's Inspired Latinas!"

Jacqueline Camacho-Ruiz
Today's Inpired Latina Founder. Author of The Little Book of Business Secrets that Work, The Fig Factor, The Fig Factor Journal, 200 Consejos Poderosos para Alcanzar el Éxito en los Negocios, Overcoming Mediocrity contributing author, and The Crusaders comic book superhero character.

Preface

LUISA ACOSTA-FRANCO

VP/Head of Recruitment Marketing & Field Support –
Farmers Insurance

I have always believed that strong women not only lift each other up, but achieve success when they help others succeed. I have been blessed throughout my career to be mentored and sponsored by some extremely talented women; women who are not afraid to empower others and share their connections to help them succeed.

Some of the most successful women I know became who they are by building others up. It's these women that I call "connectors" because they help others connect in a meaningful way to help us all prosper. It is a skill that I am proud to have learned from some of these great women. It is this skill that brought me to Jackie Camacho-Ruiz.

I first met Jackie through a mutual friend, Gabriela Reyna, a successful agency owner with Farmers Insurance Group. I had asked Gabby to speak on a panel for Women's History Month at the annual HOPE Latina History Day Conference in Los Angeles. I wanted to bring in another talented Latina to speak about entrepreneurship. Gabby raved about Jackie and immediately set up a call for us.

There was an instant affinity between Jackie and myself because we both believed in the power of mentorship and connection. Since that day, we have continued to stay in touch, often helping each other make connections with others, doing what we can for young people as role models and mentors, and always picking up where we left off in our last conversation.

Volume III of "Today's Inspired Latina" is all about connecting. It is through these stories of inspiration, challenges and successes that we connect on a deeper and meaningful level. They reinstate my belief that Latinas are growing and becoming a louder voice in business and higher education, as well as a more powerful force in this country's economic growth. Jackie and the ladies in this book all know that real power lies in building others up, and that working together, sharing each other's stories, connecting and being inclusive is the only way to foster successful connections. We must remember that behind every successful woman is a loyal tribe of "mujeres" that have supported, empowered, and connected her to others to get her to her place. It's this tribe that will also have her back.

Jackie, we got your back! *Adelante Amiga!*

Minué Yoshida

"Your mission will chase you and find you."

There are people who know what they want to be from an early age. They have a clear vision in their minds and if you ask them what they want to be, they immediately respond "fireman" or "teacher." I was never one of those people.

Growing up as the youngest of four children, I didn't have a clue about what I wanted to be. But I quickly discovered **what I wanted to DO.**

As a small girl in Mexico City, I was watching a television program featuring men and women wearing the dazzling traditional dresses of the different regions of the country. Performing in France, they were proudly representing our country through the ballet of Amalia Hernandez. *¡Que belleza, que orgullo!* Even now, a few decades later when I see it again, I am still mesmerized by the beauty and perfection of the dancers. I remember thinking "ok, this is what I want to do when I grow up." I didn't know the name of the profession or the exact job; I just knew I had to do something bigger than me, something about sharing cultures around the world, about tolerance, respect, acceptance, and embracing multiculturalism. I didn't know then that this was my mission; now I understand it as my calling.

We all have a calling; something we are amazing at, something that comes easy for us, something we are born to do, a gift, *un don, un regalo de Dios.* And the sooner we allow that mission to guide our path, the sooner we'll discover happiness. This is the story of how my mission chased me and found me. I know for sure that your mission will do the same to you. **The sooner you recognize the signs and embrace your mission, the sooner you'll find happiness, freedom, and purpose.** Here is how it happens.

YOUR MISSION WHISPERS TO YOU

Listen to the signs around you.

When I was young and trying to figure out what I wanted to do with my life, my mom hired a vocational coach. After administering some tests, he told me what I already knew, "You can do anything, because you like everything." Thanks for the news.

The end of my high school was approaching like an out of control train. My father garnered international recognition for his extensive pediatric research. We were invited to a very sophisticated restaurant, and had a private dinner with some very important people (so I was told, I still don't remember their names).

One of the hosts asked me the question dreaded by all directionless high school seniors, "What are you going to study in college?"

Since I must have had a panicked, confused look on my face, he asked me what I enjoyed doing most. Ok, I can answer that. I told him I wanted to do something for the world, where I could help others and make sure justice always prevailed. I cannot believe how ambitiously ambiguous that sounds now!

For some reason, he took pity on me and my uncertainty. Giving me his business card, he told me, "You are a very smart girl, from a brilliant lineage. I know you'll go far. I think you would be a great lawyer and so you should focus on international law. When you do, call me; I'll hire you." Since that was the only option in my confused mind, I pursued that path the very next year.

I applied to the best universities in Mexico City. The Universidad Panamericana called and said they had good news and bad news. The bad news was that I passed the law exam, but enrollment was closed. The good news was that I could enroll in the School of Pedagogy (education), and in six months, automatically switch to law. And so, with my newfound direction, I began my college career. I thought, "Six months will fly by." Little did I know **about the relationship between mission and destiny.**

The first day of classes, we had six teachers, all of them PhDs, authors, and experts on topics ranging from psychology to law. One of those teachers, Dr. Maria Pliego, offered some insight similar to this:

Education is the key to all the doors in the world. We define it as finding the potential of human beings, and bringing them towards their level of perfection. Education starts at conception and ends with our last breath. We learn and educate ourselves and others, every day, and it's the way to move from existence to transcendence.

The world stopped spinning as she was speaking; I was mesmerized. She finished, and with my eyes wide open, I smiled broadly. **My path had been revealed to me.** I had fallen madly in love with our human potential.

After graduation, I worked in the operations and processes department for an international company. My job was to travel to the U.S., learn and record their methodology, then bring the "know how" to Mexico. This job was second nature to me since I had always thought in terms of flow charts and to-do-lists. Soon I was asked to *explain* a few of those processes to my other colleagues, and before I knew it, I was in the training department!

Soon they asked if I would be willing to take over the training manager position for the office in Monterrey, Nuevo Leon. Although it meant leaving my friends, family, and city, I jumped right into this new challenge. What a life-shaping choice! My ten-trainer team was the best, both personally and professionally. In fact, I still talk to them and would work with them in a snap. In those days, **my mission was whispering to me.**

After a few years, I had so much to give. My "fish tank" was not big enough. So, when another company offered my next challenge in Mexico City, I accepted immediately. This time, I was leading the membership retention and quality department for a U.S. company throughout Latin America. We ran operations in different countries, launched successful programs, including a comprehensive certification program in three languages, and found interactive ways to help others learn a skill, improve their abilities, and expand their horizons. Once again, I was training. I was helping others find their light.

YOUR MISSION EMERGES

It's true. Your mission will find you.

My mission started to manifest in one of its purest ways: through traveling to different countries and learning other languages. It was one of my finest work experiences. The people I met, the ones who worked beside me, and the ones I left in other countries all became part of my dream and my life mission before I realized it.

Then my life changed again. After finding my loving life companion, we got married and bought our first house in Virginia. Undaunted by moving to a new country and culture, I started working in another division of the same company. This time, I was supporting member services, focusing on user interaction and customer experience in the U.S. and Mexico. In a few years, I became part of a selective group of international managers. Very soon, I was helping establish the training program for diverse groups, teaching others, and speaking in public. **My mission pursued me to another country!**

After three years, once again pursuing an opportunity, I found myself in New York working for the largest advertising and marketing group in the world, as a consultant for diverse Fortune 100 companies. I enjoyed finding sales and services gaps, ways to improve their revenue, areas of opportunities from hiring, and recruiting profiles to compensation and product lines. And as the fates would have it, I ended up doing these three things: training, development, and public speaking. I guess you can see the trend now.

After four years, a friend told me a financial company needed someone with my skills, knowledge, and experience, focused in the Hispanic market. Since I was co-founder of the Latino Employee Resource Group in the advertising company, I thought this new job was perfect. Later on, I expanded to all the multicultural markets in the U.S. I was thrilled to be working my dream job.

For many years, I learned about leadership, diversity and inclusion, and multicultural marketing from amazing people. Most importantly, **I learned about myself.**

Since 2010, I've been featured as the keynote speaker for many events at prestigious companies, colleges, and universities. It is the people I meet at each event that mean the most to me. They wait in line to talk and connect with me. I have people laughing, yelling, and crying at my sessions. I am able to touch their thoughts and feelings, and they touch mine.

On 2012, people started asking me, "Did you bring your book with you? Could you sign it?" And all I could respond is "Sure, it's on its way." I needed to start typing ASAP!

My friend and colleague, who started a large group for Latinas, started inviting me to speak in Chicago, New York, Florida, Washington, and for many Global Fortune 100 companies. Suddenly, my mission found me! I saw it clearly: help others feel inspired and take action.

RECOGNIZE YOUR MISSION

When you find your mission, embrace it and stop running from it.

My position in my company was eliminated. I searched for an option internally and externally, but all were limited in creativity, innovation, and territory. So, for the first time, I listened to myself, I followed my heart, and decided to be loyal to my calling: **to put myself in places and situations where I can help others shine, with their own light.**

For a few months, I felt something squeezing me, crushing me and making me quit! I thought it was despair, anger, or anguish. Instead, it was **my mission hugging me in joy,** embracing me like my precious eight-year-old boy when I come back home from traveling.

With nothing in my way, I stopped running. I realized it doesn't matter how hard you run, or how well you hide, your mission **will chase you and will always find you.** So, I created my own company.

The first step in following your mission is to only listen to the positive words that make you do things. Eliminate the word "can't" from your vocabulary. Your mission can only reveal itself and be achieved if you believe it is possible.

Now, my question to you is, can you hear your calling?

If you can't, just think of something that you excel at,

something you've been doing your entire life. It could be a single thing, a series of things, or a very tactical list of things. And if you cannot recognize your own strengths, remember that our mission pursues us **by manifesting itself with tremendous clarity from others.**

Think of the something(s) that people notice and tell you, like "you should do X." "When are you doing X for a living? You are awesome at it." "Why aren't you doing X if you have the talent?"

Universal truth can allow others to see what you cannot. Let others tell you what you are amazing at and start doing it!

Once you find yourself traveling the path of your mission, **you have one more obligation: pass it on.** When you see someone as lost as you once were, help them stop running from their mission.

Your mission is like the Olympic torch; once it touches you (and it will) you'll have no choice but to take it, start running, and find someone to whom you can pass it on. **The crystal clear signs are all there.** Stop running from what you are supposed to do and run with it!

REFLECTION

1. Do you believe you have a mission in life? What is it?

2. What do people say are your greatest talents?

3. Do you feel you are running away from your mission? Why? What can you do about that?

BIOGRAPHY

Minué Yoshida is President of Yoshida Consulting and is an international speaker, public speaking coach, multicultural guru, and wonder woman! Born and raised in Mexico City to a Mexican mother and Japanese father, Minué has a unique understanding of how leveraging the strengths of a multicultural environment can enhance organizations.

Minué has more than 20 years of experience in training, sales, marketing, and communications. Working with Fortune 100 companies in the U.S., Mexico, Brazil, Argentina, and Puerto Rico, she has developed and implemented programs to grow their profitability, increase social impact, and enchant customers through leadership development, and multicultural and multi-generational inclusion.

Fluent in English, Spanish, and Portuguese (with knowledge of French and Japanese), Minué holds degrees in business education pedagogy from the Universidad Panamericana, Mexico, and in professional leadership skills development from the Universidad Iberoamericana, Mexico. Additionally, she earned several professional certifications in training and public speaking as well as life and health licensing from the Chartered Leadership Fellowship (American College, USA).

Minué delivers workshops on leadership development, public speaking, and is a featured speaker on diversity and inclusion. She

 has been active in professional Latino advancement, Asian network leadership, and LGTB groups as well as professional women's empowerment initiatives and organizations.

Minué Yoshida
minue@yoshidaconsulting.com
(212) 699-0659

Belisa Perez

"Use what God has given you, add faith, put in the work and declare your victory."

I was born in Queens, New York and I had the perfect life – or at least I thought so when I was a child. My parents, both immigrants from Honduras, came to this country along with my two older brothers to seek a better life. My mom always tells me I was long awaited because for about seven years, she couldn't conceive. She claims that deep inside she knew the day I was conceived that I was going to be a girl. She was right.

MY STORY BEGINS

I grew up in a Christian home and we went to church every Sunday. I enjoyed attending Sunday school because it would bring the bible stories to life and I began to discover my love of singing during worship time. My mother also says that when I was four, I would sing worship songs on the train as we traveled. There was no doubt that I was gifted in that area-- I got it from my daddy. He used to love to sing and I can vividly remember him singing to me this one particular native Honduran song – "*Candu, "Negrita para amarte, nació mi corazón*" ("little brown-skinned girl, my heart was born to love you."). Although he wasn't very affectionate, he showed me love as he knew how. I could do no wrong in his eyes and he spoiled me.

I remember being a content 15-year-old in my second year of high school. I considered myself friendly, yet a little reserved, because I had secret insecurities. During this time, I was proudly part of a youth group and sang in the worship team. Although I was taught that God loved me, I didn't always believe it. Deep inside, I wanted to believe and walk in my faith but there were things and experiences from my childhood that didn't let me move on. Little did I know that the following decisions I'd make that year would change my life forever.

In 1995, I met someone I thought was the love of my life. We talked about a future together and vowed to do things right before God, our family, and everyone, until… that moment when we put ourselves in a dead-end position. In a nutshell, I became pregnant, got married, and moved out within a matter of months. On April 20, 1996 at the age of 16, I gave birth to a baby boy. Thankfully, I had the full support of my family. That's when I really learned that love has no boundaries. I was truly experiencing God's love through their support. I also felt guilty and like a failure for not living up to everyone's expectations for me, including my own. I was always the girl to stand up for what I believed in. Sharing my faith and even encouraging young girls to abstain from sex until marriage was the norm, and there I was, a teen mom. I decided to move on with my head held high. I always knew God had a great purpose for my life and I was ready to do what it took. But it was a constant struggle with my brokenness. It wasn't easy. After having to move to Puerto Rico for three years and battling many trials, my husband and I decided to separate and then got divorced. It was one of the hardest things I've ever had to do.

SOW AND REAP

God is in the business of restoration and that's exactly what began in my life as I returned to NYC. I had faith that it would bring healing for my future. The idea of starting college was surreal and I decided to pursue a career in business and information systems. I began to faithfully attend church and God was dealing with the pain of my past. My life was filled with hope, and a divine opportunity for love arose. I met my love, friend, husband, and the father of my three children. We also went through a process and a waiting period before we got married, but it's been almost 11 years, and we're blessed by friends, family, and most importantly, God.

As I think about these last couple of years, I can't help but be completely thankful for the major breakthroughs in all areas of my life – in my personal growth, my marriage, as a mom, in ministry, and in business! God placed my husband and me in leadership over a ministry which was a treat because we began to invest and pour ourselves in other people's lives, and we saw Him at work. It hasn't always been easy but when you ask God to take you to the next level, expect to be tried and stretched. Your heart will be tested! The key is to endure even when things don't make sense, trusting that the Holy Spirit is at work.

After I had my daughters, I developed a passion for building a business and I did. I had no idea what I was doing and opened up an online boutique for little girls. During that time, I had both girls in daycare while I worked a full-time job and when I realized that I could potentially replace my income, I quit. Then I learned about affiliate marketing and started to invest in myself to learn more. I built several teams online while selling other people's digital products.

One of the things I'm passionate about is helping women, especially moms like me, overcome their limiting beliefs when they feel stuck, so they can apply their faith to go after their dreams and build a business and life they love. This was a self-discovery journey for me though. Things began to surface as I moved forward, and I needed to confront things in my past that were hindering me from moving forward.

As I became more aligned to what I knew God was calling me to do, the stretching process began again. I always shied away from public speaking and exposing myself to crowds, and that's exactly where I was being called. If I wanted God to grow me, I needed to be visible, start speaking, become vulnerable and share my story. This meant getting uncomfortable, embracing it, and so I started to prepare. There's always a price to pay! You can't live your life expecting doors to automatically open up for you. There will be times where you're going to have to make moves, insert the keys you were born with, turn knobs, and open doors yourself. It's going to mean that you have to invest time, money, sweat, and tears.

When God calls you and tells you to go, it's time to go! Things will never be perfect and the money won't always be right. Focus on making moves and getting started instead of waiting for perfection. This is how I boldly started to make connections and share my gifts and talents with others to serve them with vision crafting, branding, social media, and online business building.

When you plan according to God's direction for your life, He's going to back you up, open doors, close doors, clear the way, and bless you far beyond anything you've ever imagined! Most importantly, He's going to bless your generations because of the seeds you are sowing today! Learn to build relationships, add value, and be real. It may take time, but keep sowing on fertile ground and you will see the fruit of your alignment, obedience, and labor.

Lastly, say YES to new adventures--life is short. Maybe it's travel, a career, business, ministry, or even a degree. If you're aligned with God's vision for your life, you can't miss the opportunities He places before you. Sow and you will reap!

FINISH WHAT YOU START

There are no limits to what you can accomplish in life. If you follow your God-given vision and dream, you can make it a reality. Many of us have been programmed to have a limited mindset but we can reframe our thoughts and be open to expansion. I felt like that about completing my college degree.

I stopped going to school for about seven years and only had about three classes left but I decided to focus on taking care of my babies. It has been a journey! My girls were both in school full-time and I was so close to graduating that it made sense to do it. It's not about telling your children how to live life, but showing them. Another reason I did it was that I had a bad habit of starting things and not completing them. To be frank, it was just hard to pay the price! Also, I'm often afraid of the responsibility that completion brings. After doing some inner work, I decided to break that in my life! I was going to fearlessly move forward.

No matter what battle you face, use what God has given you. Add faith, put in the work and declare your victory! If God gave you His word (knowledge, wisdom, resources, tactic, strategy, etc.), use it. And if you lack these, ask and you shall receive. I thank God for surrounding me with supportive and uplifting people who showed up with divine appointments! Remember, you can pick up where you left off. Follow your calling and be intentional. I'm proud to say that I finally obtained my BS in Information Systems Management.

I believe IDENTITY + PURPOSE = a THRIVING LIFE. I believe we were all created in the image of God. We carry His identity and He created us with purpose and for purpose. However, we have to accept our identity in order to truly walk in our purpose. Only then can we be in full alignment and truly live a thriving life. God knew exactly what He was doing when He created you. It doesn't matter how broken you've been. You were not created to live in pain. He gave you beauty for ashes but you have to embrace it and walk in it.

Not everyone will encourage and support you but don't

let anyone convince you that you can't move forward and change things around for yourself. You just read snippets of my experiences, and if I overcame, you are enough to overcome! Don't let self-limiting beliefs keep you from taking action on your God-given dreams.

If a lack of confidence is something you need to overcome, keep your eyes on your goal. Draw closer to God and connect with people that inspire you to be a better you! I wasn't always confident and there are even some days now that I feel insecure. I remind myself that I am secure in God, and my power and confidence comes from Him. I challenge you to dig deep to seek growth. Once you begin to see God's hand in your life, you will know that his workmanship in you and through you was uniquely made just for you. His perfect design for your life pulls together every thread of who you are into a magnificent masterpiece.

As you take bold steps, take consistent small steps and keep the end goal in mind. You may not know where God will lead you next, but know that He wants you to Dream, Play BIG and Thrive! Be willing to fail and never give up.

Finally, Go ALL IN with life. Don't be afraid to overcommit and make sure you over-deliver. Dream, Do, and take others with you. Today, I celebrate my journey. I had a rough start, but I'm determined, hopeful, and most of all, grateful. It's time to allow prayer, purpose, hard work, and dedication to come into fulfillment.

REFLECTION

1. Have you honored your past in order to heal and embrace your future? Are you living your life to its fullest potential despite your past failures?

2. Have you accepted your God-given identity? What do you think is your purpose in life?

3. How are you making connections to build solid relationships that will help you succeed?

BIOGRAPHY

Belisa Perez is an Inspirational Mompreneur – a Mindset and Online Business Coach who helps purpose-driven women create powerful brands and build profitable, online businesses they love.

She is passionate about empowering women to release the limiting beliefs and mindset blocks that keep them from success and living their own dreams and purpose. She's a certified speaker, published author, social media coach and founder of the online community, Kingdom Mompreneurs Unite (www.KingdomMompreneurs.com).

Belisa is one of the collaborating authors in the best-selling book, *Journey to the Stage Vol. 3* that can be obtained at www.BelisaSpeaks. com. She has been featured in Empowering Women TV & Radio, iStand TV, the Women's Prosperity Network – NYC chapter, and was one of the "Leading Latinas en New York 2016." Belisa is currently the Digital Tribe Communications Specialist for The Business of WE, a digital platform for women entrepreneurs. She was recently featured in *Strong and Courageous Women Magazine*.

Belisa holds a Bachelor of Science degree in Information Systems Management and is an Associate Pastor alongside her husband at Iglesia Cristiana El Buen Samaritano (Good Samaritan Christian Church) in NYC where they live with their three children.

Belisa Perez
www.belisaperez.com
(347) 451-3892

Tamika Lecheé Morales

"In the end, we're all stories but it's what you do with
your story that matters."

It's easy to brag about the beauty of motherhood, but rarely do we share our struggles with it. Why is that? Is it because we're embarrassed or just afraid of being judged? I am going to get vulnerable with you in hopes that I can bring awareness about a cause that has become near and dear to my heart.

Motherhood has been the hardest thing I've ever had to endure; harder than growing up poor, harder than growing up without my mother, harder than knowing that I will never meet my father, and worse, that he will never even know I exist.

As a young mother, I wished that there was an instruction manual on how to raise children. I often felt guilty for not doing more, or not always being present as I tried to balance pursuing my own aspirations and career with raising my children.

Yet everything I did was not only for me, but for my family. I never wanted my kids to endure the heartache that I felt as a child, so I sacrificed to give them what I never had. Unfortunately, the universe had a funny way of reminding me that we are not always in control, and that sometimes God has a bigger plan for our lives than we do.

FOREVER CHANGED

It was June 4, 2015, a day like any other for most people. But for me, it was the day that ripped my heart out. We were sitting in a medical office, observing Maximillian, our nearly five-year-old son. He was undergoing an evaluation recommended by his preschool. We watched as therapists asked him a seemingly infinite number of questions.

"Where does a bird live?"

"What's the plural of this?"

"What's the opposite of that?"

"What's the noun in this sentence?"

"Fish is to water as bird is to…?"

The questions went on forever. I couldn't help but think, "Is a four-year-old really expected to know the answers to all of these questions?", but I cheered him on internally whenever he answered correctly. I was amazed at how much he knew. Then after sitting for nearly 45 minutes, Maximillian became restless. He wanted to be done. I was concerned that he wouldn't cooperate as the evaluators tried creatively to engage him and get the last of their answers.

Then the parent survey began.

"Does your child prefer to play with other children or on his own?"

"Does he look into your eyes when you speak to him?"

"Does he engage in pretend play?"

After nearly two grueling hours, my husband Hugo and I were anxiously waiting for the doctor to review the results of

Maximillian's evaluation. We were quiet in the waiting room while our son searched through the toy box. I saw his innocent excitement as he found cars to play with. My mind raced. I was lost in my thoughts trying to make my own assessments and convincing myself that our son was "*normal*."

At last, the doctor walked in and formally introduced herself. After asking more questions, she said the words that pierced right through my heart, causing it to shatter into a million little pieces. "Diagnosis: Autism Spectrum Disorder (ASD) and Attention Deficit Hyperactivity Disorder (ADHD)."

I looked at my son and fought back the tears by clenching my fists and squeezing my fingernails into the palm of my hands (a trick that someone taught me to avoid crying) but the tears seeped in anyway. I quickly began to blink away the mist so that no one noticed my sorrow. I REFUSED TO CRY. NOT THERE, NOT THEN. I WANTED TO BE STRONG.

I immediately wanted to know if my son could be "cured" of this diagnosis and asked the doctor if it was possible to overcome autism. She was very frank and said that doing so was extremely rare, and most people still showed remnants of the disorder, specifically with their social behaviors. I kept repeating to her, "But it is possible then?" She tried to tell me in various ways that most children with autism will forever live with the disorder. She didn't want to give me a false sense of hope, but I just wanted to hear something that was optimistic and could mend my broken heart.

The doctor began talking about resources or something and

I tuned out. I got lost in my head. Then it happened. A tear escaped and began to roll down my cheek; then another down my chin. I wanted to scream "WHY?! GOD, WHY ME?! WHAT HAVE I DONE TO DESERVE THIS?"

The doctor exited the room to give us a moment. Then my husband, without meaning to, upset me even more by asking me something like, "How you holding up?" I couldn't help but think "Are you serious? What kind of stupid f***ing question is that? Is that really the best you can come up with?" But in all fairness, I don't think either one of us knew how to respond in that moment to what we just heard. And I just remember being furious at both him and God, and thinking God was "punishing me" for something.

That night, like every other night, Maximillian climbed on my chest to fall asleep. But this time, when I rocked him to sleep, I held him tightly and cried. I vowed NOT to share Maximillian's diagnosis with anyone, not even his brother, Sebastian, or the rest of our family and friends. I made my husband promise not to share it with anyone either.

For a long time after that, I felt alone. I wouldn't talk about what I was feeling with anyone, not even my husband. I found myself going through all the stages of grief (disbelief, denial, bargaining, guilt, anger, depression, and acceptance/hope). After Maximillian's diagnosis, we had him tested to rule out any genetic causes of autism, like Fragile X Syndrome (the most common genetic cause of ASD). After the results came in, a genetic counselor told us: "His autism is not genetic, therefore, it's environmental." My mind went crazy with possibilities. At one point, I even blamed myself for his autism and wondered if I caused it during my pregnancy. Did I eat wrong? Exercise too much? Take the wrong type of vitamins? I had even delayed most of his vaccines to ensure that he didn't get more than one vaccine at a time because of the controversy linked with autism and vaccinations. I finally came to the realization that whatever it was, I just had to come to terms with it and accept it.

FEARS ARE STORIES WE TELL OURSELVES

I think I didn't share what I was going through because I feared people would regard my son as inferior, or worse, that they would feel sorry for me. I didn't want people's pity and I definitely didn't want people's judgment. Intentionally or unintentionally, when we put labels on people, we contribute to stereotypes, and disseminate misinformation. It's usually due to a lack of education. We only educate ourselves on things that matter to us.

At the same time, I know that we can't fault people for their ignorance. Usually, we're just naïve to the things that don't affect us. I am guilty of that. My awareness of autism became relevant because of my son's diagnosis. Before that, I didn't know enough about it so I feared it. Therefore, I feared telling others.

"Your ego is not your amigo," especially when it comes to matters of the heart. I knew that I had to surrender myself completely and take my ego out of it. Only then could I comprehend how I really wasn't helping myself, or more importantly, my son. I also had to forgive myself. I began sharing my despair with others and I began to get help, ideas, and resources.

Little by little, the feeling of hopelessness began to dissipate. While autism is just one aspect of Maximillian's character, it doesn't define him. When I educated myself on autism, I began to realize how incredible autistic children actually were. In fact, many studies show that autistic children have extraordinary gifts and prodigies share certain genetic traits with those who have autism, such as exceptional memories and attention to detail. Many of them even overcome their social deficits with intensive interventions. Learning this helped me overcome my fear of embarrassment and judgment. I began sharing my son's diagnosis with a selected few, including our family, and educating them on autism so they too wouldn't fear it.

SIMPLE THINGS WE TAKE FOR GRANTED

Maximillian doesn't participate in several events due to his autism. At times, he lacks self-control and can't remain silent. He has a habit of singing and regurgitating cartoon shows and commercials even while he does his school work. It's how he copes. I often get emails and calls from his school teachers about his various impulses. It takes Maximillian longer to learn certain things than most children his age, like tying his shoelaces, getting himself dressed, and wiping his bottom. Also, making friends and socializing are a real challenge because of his unique mannerisms. He doesn't understand boundaries and has yet to master the art of proper play and engaging in meaningful conversations.

Maximillian also has eating issues. He wouldn't eat anything that wasn't pizza, rice, crackers, noodle soup, or chocolate when he was younger. I was desperate for him to eat anything other than carbs and junk food. He was undernourished, and was not taking in the vitamins and minerals he needed to be healthy. He'd scream and cry when we introduced other foods into his diet, and still does.

Thankfully, we were able to start Maximillian on an intensive intervention program that included all types of therapies: developmental, occupational, speech, food and Applied Behavioral Analysis (ABA). These therapies assisted Maximillian greatly. After a full day at school, he continues therapy for three arduous hours daily. It is taxing on all of us, but especially him. While other kids are in soccer, karate, or some other recreational activity, he is learning how to socialize appropriately, use his fine-motor skills, express himself, and eat various foods. Maximillian is very bright. In Kindergarten, he already read very well, but within the year he was reading fluently in two languages because we placed him in a bilingual program. He was able to count money, tell time, use a very advanced vocabulary, add and subtract double digits, and more. However, he continues to struggle socially, and follow certain instructions. It's been a very hard road but we continue to dedicate all the resources he needs to succeed.

We're so grateful for the remarkable and hard-working teachers and therapists who are devoted to Maximillian. I am also so appreciative to Maximillian's babysitter Gabby, who has loved and cared for Maximillian since he was six-weeks-old. I have never seen a bond like theirs before and I should be jealous, but instead my heart is full of love for her. Gabby was God-sent, as was the beautiful Sylvia. I had no means of getting Maximillian from school to Gabby's house because Gabby doesn't drive. Sylvia had worked with Maximillian as his bilingual translator during therapy and generously offered to drive him to Gabby after school. I have never met two more generous souls who would do anything for Maximillian. They are blessings from above, as is the amazing network of friends and family in our lives.

People who have not been exposed to children with special needs can never fully comprehend the magnitude of what it takes to care for them, physically and emotionally. Having to endure the challenges of ADHD with my oldest son Sebastian was strenuous enough, but this new challenge doesn't even compare. Nevertheless, our boys are our world and I know that God has his own plan for us with the lessons we're humbly learning.

Maximillian has made serious strides but we still go through the challenges of raising a son with autism. Dealing with people's ignorance can be one of the most exhausting parts of this odyssey: the labels, the stereotypes, the endless judgement, the constant justifications and apologies for the way Maximillian behaves, and the certain things he does. We also worry that Maximillian could be bullied and constantly find ourselves advocating for him.

But what I find hardest to deal with is not knowing what the future holds for my son. Will Maximillian have true friends?

Will he be able to drive and live on his own? Will he be able to take care of himself and have a career? Will he get married and have children? These are the things "normal" people take for granted and it troubles me to think that Maximillian may never be able to experience them. It is painful to accept, especially because of how generously loving he is.

Not a day goes by that he doesn't tell me he loves me, or that I am his best friend, or even sweeter, when he says, "Mommy, you are my sunshine." He truly makes my heart melt. Even now that we force him to sleep in his own bed, not a night goes by that he doesn't sneak into my bed to cuddle up with me in the middle of the night. As I began to accept his diagnosis, I also began to realize that a lot of the qualities that I loved about him were probably a result of his condition. That was when I decided to embrace his autism, see the beauty in it, and become a voice for autism awareness.

CHANGE YOUR STORY

My life stories propelled me to become a playwright. In sharing them, I hope to raise awareness, evoke consciousness, and inspire others. I realized that there was power in getting vulnerable and sharing my story, because it is not just my story; it is our story. It's when we share our stories that we *all* find healing. When I decided to focus on the beauty in my son's autism, everything changed. Maximillian's story inspired me to write my next play, *For the Love of Autism*.

I encourage you to share your story so that we can learn

from one another, discover resources, find our voice, and activate others. Don't let your story die within you. No matter what you've been through, only you have the power to wake up tomorrow and change your story. In the end, we're all stories but it's what you do with *your story* that matters.

REFLECTION

1. What do you need to accept in order to forgive yourself and move forward?

2. We're all stories in the end. What story do you NEED to share that can help others?

3. "Who lives; who dies; and who tells your story?" What will be your legacy and how will you share it?

BIOGRAPHY

Tamika Lecheé Morales is a fiery "Nuyorican", full of energy and passion. She lives for her two sons, Sebastian (22) and Maximillian (6), and for exotic vacations with her sexy man, Hugo, who she has loved for more than 23 years.

She is a second grade, dual language teacher and is passionate about helping her students become bilingual, biliterate, and bicultural.

Tamika is also an actress and serves humanity by raising cultural awareness, invoking thought, and raising consciousness in the hearts and minds of audiences. Hence, she began sharing her life stories as a playwright. She is currently producing her first play, *The Nuyorican*, about breaking the vicious cycle of a broken childhood, and is writing her next play, *For the Love of Autism*.

Tamika is a company member with UrbanTheater Company and Halcyon Theatre. She is also a co-host on *Inspira TeVe* and former owner of a Liberty Tax Service, which she still manages part-time.

Recently, Tamika was invited to serve as president of the board and as an ambassador for "The Autism Hero Project", a not-for-profit organization that creates awareness and acceptance while celebrating children with autism.

She is also the past vice president of the Puerto Rican Heritage Organization and choreographer for their scholarship pageants.

Tamika Lecheé Morales
tamika.l.morales@gmail.com
(847) 909-8740

Margarita Duque

"Fulfill your dreams with love and faith."

First of all, I'd like to thank God the almighty who has given me the strength and courage to reach all of my dreams. By his grace, I am walking into another chapter in my life, and for that I am thankful! God you are good!

Be authentic and follow your heart. Fulfill your dreams with love and faith; they will take you to a successful path. What works for others may not work for you; what works for you, might not work for others. Seek your own applause and not the applause of others.

AN UNEXPECTED HOME

My journey began in October 1992 when I arrived in Chicago with my wonderful 9-year-old daughter Evelyn to reunite with her father, who was my husband at the time. The purpose of the trip was not to stay in the United States permanently but to return with my family to Quito, Ecuador. (Those were my plans, but God's plans were completely different.)

After a month of living in Chicago, I started working at an assembly factory through a temporary agency. Some days I was called to work and others I was simply sent back home. I didn't have my own transportation and always found someone in the factory that could give me a ride. My strength came from wanting to become independent and provide a better lifestyle for my daughter.

We lived in an apartment with my ex-husband's relatives but I wanted to save enough money to rent our own apartment, so that our daughter would feel loved and welcomed in her own home. My desire to change my lifestyle was greater than anything I could imagine; I was willing to do whatever it took to change our future, even if it meant working two jobs every day. Finally, I reached my goal and we moved into our own apartment.

When my daughter and I arrived in Chicago, it was cold and cloudy, just like the people we were living with. Tension began to escalate between us. We were living with people who didn't have any respect for others, and were full of envy, very pessimistic, and without family values. It was unbearable to see my daughter in pain caused by her family members and hard for me because I come from a family where we love and respect each other.

Back in Ecuador, I had a very good position and an excellent salary as a chief administrative assistant. I was surrounded by prestigious professionals. In no way did it ever cross my mind to move and look for other employment opportunities. Now, even though I was starting from the bottom, everything I did to achieve my goals and have a better life I did with an inner peace and without questioning all the adversities. My heart never felt pain; my only desire was to have a better life for my family. Today as I am remembering my past, writing this chapter of my life, I can say that God was my life coach. God began to train me and strengthen me in all the areas of my life. As God's word says, "He already knew me even before I was in my mother's womb; the Lord had and has plans for me and for you!"

In the factory I was surrounded by people with different nationalities and very diverse cultures, however the Hispanic culture prevailed. I started to make a very above-average salary, receiving around $500 a week. My aspirations grew. I wanted to buy my first car and a house.

In my heart and mind I did not feel satisfied with my workplace. It was not the income that gave me these second thoughts on leaving my job as supervisor of the group in my section. I loved working there and I loved the people, especially those from India, who accepted me as part of them. Our bond became strong and they shared their Hindu culture with me. They taught me certain words in Urdu, and invited me to their most personal and cultural festivities, like baby and wedding showers, etc. Yet every day I grew more and more impatient to achieve something greater for my life.

FACING FEAR WITH FAITH

When fear comes upon you, you start having a war with yourself, having doubts about your abilities and the fear of failure. It is not easy! I decided to embrace my fears and make them part of who I am. I dominated fear through the faith that God would open opportunities for me through people and job offers. I was presented with the opportunity to meet a person who worked as a supervisor in an insurance company, which at that time was the largest insurance company in the Hispanic market. I asked this person for an opportunity to join the company. I completed the application, waited six months and did not receive a call from the agency.

One day, I decided to go to the agency myself to ask about the position and they told me they never received the application. Right there, in the office, I completed another application. Three months passed, and I kept calling with the faith and hope that they would take time to interview me, however I was always advised to call back another time. I kept calling, but after a while, I was ready to give up and just stay where I was. Thankfully, the last time I called, I was told, "Alright, I'll wait for you tomorrow for an interview. I'm very intrigued to meet the persistent person who keeps calling for the position. You do not even have the adequate language skills, yet it is not deterring you from becoming a better you!"

I was so excited. I arrived the next morning for the interview and without hesitation they congratulated me with the new job. The beginning salary was five dollars an hour, which was much less than the income I was currently receiving at the factory. I asked myself, "Is this what you really want? You're going to earn much less, and it will not be enough income to support the household." There were so many thoughts running through my mind. I had no idea what I was going to do.

As I arrived home, I shared my concern with the father of my two children and asked if he would support my decision if I took this opportunity. He replied, "We'll see what happens." Despite his response, I decided to take the risk and accept the opportunity that I had wanted for so long.

I started in the filing department. I wanted to show this company that I could accomplish more so I kept reminding myself that it doesn't matter where I start; it is more important to show who I am and how I am capable of reaching my goals. This was the opportunity that I had looked for and I was going to make the best of it. I thanked God for all of it. Gratitude, humility, and spiritual principles will get you out of your concerns, and faith will lift you up! Everything we ask in the name of Jesus, we will receive!

Two weeks later, the president of the company called me and told me that as of the following month I would be receiving a dollar raise and training for customer service. Again, fear came upon me. I was nervous because of my language skills. Luckily, the majority of our customers were Hispanic. I completed my tasks with responsibility, love, gratitude, and dedication. I gave it my all; I worked more hours than I had to without expecting a reward.

After only two months as a customer service representative, I was trained to begin a new, challenging position as an insurance sales representative. Everything happened so quickly. I was astonished that I was accomplishing all these challenges in such a short time frame. I started selling car insurance and a year after,

I became the top sales agent in the company. My production alone was equivalent to that of five other sales agents. It was definitely not easy to achieve that position because I had to deal with people's insecurities which generated envy, selfishness, and wicked actions with the intent of getting me fired from the company. Their negativity never stopped me. I kept setting higher goals, doing my best and every year for me was more and more successful. I would fulfill the company's annual goals, but I was also reaching my own, which were much higher than the ones the company set.

My dreams were turning into reality. I bought my house and a brand new car. Most importantly, I wanted another child and was ready to have one. I asked God to grant me a son, a wonderful son, and so God granted me my son, Anthony. I dedicated myself to him, and continued working but now just part-time as a sales agent. Unbelievably, I realized that my production was the same as when I was working full time. This led me to the conclusion that if we want to succeed, we must work smarter, not harder. God rewards us when we use our time wisely and he gives many more blessings.

As the years passed, I was the star agent for 14 consecutive years. My $145 weekly income was transformed into $2,000 or more, many times a week. I thank God for sending me angels of protection, for giving me a spirit of courage, perseverance, and decision. God put someone in my life who I trusted in and gave me all his support and affection, defended me against all injustice and loved my family as his own. This person was the owner of the insurance company I was working for and I'm thankful for him because he helped launch my career as an insurance agent. Thank you Craig Lamm!

THE DECISION

I had reached a professional and economic position where I was regularly known and recognized. After a few years, I was presented with a new challenge. In the middle of the economic crisis of 2008, when the biggest companies were facing devastating losses, my daughter and I had to make a decision to open our own insurance agency with Farmers Insurance Group. It was not easy to embark on this new journey, but together, we made a great team. Our first year in business we qualified for the Toppers Club, which is an award for agents that have met or surpassed their life insurance sales goals.

However, by purposeful decisions full of love and priorities, Evelyn resigned as a Farmers Agent and I was now alone facing a new challenge with love, faith, and above all, gratitude. God has rewarded me, not only in the materialistic aspect of life but also with spiritual success. Today I count on the support of my son Anthony, my daughter Evelyn, and my husband Roberto, whom I married five years ago.

I have made all my decisions based upon my faith and God's power, not my fear. Today I understand that the presence of God was always along my path. He has given me so many gifts, especially the gift of giving without expecting anything in return. God is first in my life and then my family. I contribute to the community/church and I feel blessed and grateful to God for my spiritual transformation and his fidelity.

REFLECTION

1. What is faith? What does it represent in your life?

2. How do you overcome fear in your day-to-day life?

3. What are you deeply grateful for and what are you willing to give in return? Who do you thank?

BIOGRAPHY

Margarita Duque is a woman committed to success. With more than 22 years of experience in the insurance industry, Margarita has won many awards through the years. As a Farmers Insurance Agent she has won the Toppers and Championship awards, and she excels as a top performer and has demonstrated a professional, unparalleled level of excellence. She has built strong values and principles centered on faith, education, respect, and an urgency to help the local community.

To pursue her dreams of personal growth and giving back, Margarita obtained a life coach certification from the WCC World Coaching Corporation, IAC International Association of Coaching, which she completed while raising her two children, Anthony and Evelyn. She is passionate about elevating others to their full potential through personal and spiritual development and applies this philosophy to everything she does. Margarita believes in not only guiding her clients, but exceeding their expectations.

She is originally from Quito, Ecuador and now resides in the Midwest with her family.

Margarita Duque
morbe@farmersagent.com
(773) 746-8228

Lupita Tovar

"Everything is possible when there is true focus
and a dream in the heart."

I was born in Villanueva Zacatecas, Mexico. At the age of 19, I started a clothing business in my hometown. This would be the beginning of my life as an entrepreneur, where I would learn and develop my life's vocation. My journey to becoming the kind of business person I longed to be wasn't easy, but it was rewarding.

FAMILY BUSINESS

I am so proud of my father, because he is the man who taught me the importance of work. He would wake early in the morning, hours before I even opened my eyes, and come back to the house and shout, "Get up! It is so nice to get up early in the morning." He would arrive with jars of frothy milk because he was a farmer who took care of our cows every day, and my family sold milk, cheese and other dairy products. My mother got up very early also to sell the milk and sweep the streets. I loved the smell of wet earth when my mother watered the street - the act of throwing water onto the dusty road. At that moment, the streets came alive with the movement of the water running down to us.

My father made everything function in the house and gave us our chores, like cleaning the house and preparing the food. My mother would always ask us to embroider the napkins for the tortillas. I used to say a proverb similar in meaning to the American expression, "Time is money!" Those are the same words I repeat to my children to this day.

A jar of milk is one of the most beautiful images that I have of my childhood, when taking milk from my grandparent's house to my parent's house was the biggest challenge, yet I succeeded more than three times. My grandmother was also a beautiful example to me and she always had the best food in the world, especially her sauces, noodle soup, mole and those peach marmalades. I would patiently wait and hope for her to leave so I could quickly sneak another taste since she would only let me try one at a time.

My grandmother was a woman of ancestry, with the richest family in town, and my grandfather was a very handsome and gallant man with expressive green eyes. He was a very decent man who wouldn't even steal a nail. I remember how one of my friends who had a saddlery in the village used to laugh when recounting the story of how my grandfather had asked him for ten pesos worth of nails. After a while he returned with three in his hand, and gave them back, telling my friend that upon returning home and counting, he had realized that he had three extra nails. My grandfather had a scale in his house and would always weigh everything after he bought anything in the street. He would say, "These are your things, these belong to you."

Another friend told me how my great-grandfather Néstor returned the eggs that his neighbor's hens would lay in his corral with the same words, "These belong to you." Showing respect for others and what belongs to them was a great lesson in my life.

At one point after high school, I used to think about the parable in the bible about the bags of gold (Matthew 25: 14-30). It made me wonder what I would do if God appeared right now and asked me what I had done for Him in the time that He gave me on Earth. And from that moment on, I decided to use my gifts and my time to do something productive and worthwhile.

STEPS TO SUCCESS

When I was 19, I fell into a deep depression after I experienced a heartbreak. I felt sad and disappointed. By fate, I came across the book *The Gift of the Star* by Og Mandino and as I read it, I began to find that special light which would lead me to my own destiny. Og Mandino's book motivated me to follow certain, gradual steps to get ahead.

At the age of 22, I had great debt from my clothing store, but after deep introspection, I realized that one of the reasons was because I was letting my friends take advantage of me. Additionally, I had neglected my business, I was inexperienced as a merchant and I did not have people helping me become a better entrepreneur. When I only 19 and first starting the business, with almost no merchandise, very little money from the bank, and no support from my parents, I felt truly lost. I did not want to tell my family anything. I was terrified at the thought of them finding out how bad my financial situation was. At night I prayed for God to please help me.

On one of those desperate nights, I prayed and He sent me an angel in the form of a traveler, a vendor who offered me merchandise and gave me a month to pay him back. It was a great blessing. At that moment, I took up my work again with pleasure and pulled forward.

On one occasion, I had gone to Guadalajara to stock up on new merchandise for my store and saw that all the girls who worked there selling clothes to wholesalers looked like dress-up dolls. I began to realize that my bad habits had led me to my drastic situation and I immediately began to work on changing things. I was happy to go to work at my store every day. Thanks to my new outlook, I had a positive attitude and became an excellent seller. Besides, I always tried to look good, which not only motivated me, but my clients as well into buying my merchandise.

THE FAMILY AFFAIR

Back when I was feeling the weight of debt most heavily upon me, I was talking to a friend who made a comment that even though I had many debts, I could pay myself if I took out one big loan. With that brilliant idea in mind, I tried to take out a loan from a credit association, but it required my family to sign the papers. In addition, we had to put our house up as collateral. But how could I tell this to my father, who never even asked to borrow money for a pin in his entire life? I felt the world closing in on me. After all, I was only 20 years old.

When the credit association's manager asked for my father's signature, I claimed that he had gone to the ranch and could not go into town to sign, so I could take the papers home. After picking up the papers from the loan office, I forged my father's signature after practicing how to write it at least a million times. I snuck the papers out of his car and began to pray that my family would not find out. The credit association manager kindly turned over a check for $300,000.

With the loan, I paid my debts and with the rest, I came to the U.S. and made my way to the Los Angeles alleyways to buy clothes to take back to Mexico to sell. My parents usually picked me up at the airport when I returned from my trips, but this time something strange happened. Nobody was waiting for me. Instead, they had sent a taxi, which made me sad because I never imagined that my parents would have figured it out already. Unbeknownst to me, during my trip to the U.S., the credit association manager had asked my dad about his opinion regarding the services the association had given him. When they discovered what I had done, my family almost died of a heart attack.

Later, while I was at work, my mother came walking past the store very quickly, came inside and with a bad gesture, told me that she needed the deeds for my belongings and asked me if I had pawned my valuable goods as well. That was how I realized that my parents had learned what I had done. After she left, I began to pray as I placed the clothes that I had brought to sell from the U.S. on display in my store. When I returned home that night, my father scolded me. However, in the end he told them with an immense love that it was alright and that he would support me, but that he would not consider me a good merchant until I paid my debts. These words echoed in my heart and spirit. From then on, my purpose was to carry out that commitment, changing my habits and focusing on becoming better every day.

Time passed, and I did not falter in my goal. Eight months before the loan was due, I was already making my last payment, which earned me a discount on the interest. In that way, I filled my family with pride.

GETTING EVEN BETTER

When I was 25, I came to the U.S. and met my husband, David, where he worked at the time. With a suitcase full of dreams in our hands, and our lifetimes of experience, David and I set out on a great adventure providing popular Mexican food— not the kind you can find on any neighborhood corner (They are the kind that you find locally), but food that showcases the unique, distinctive flavors and traditions of the Latin culture.

Together, we began our biggest odyssey: starting a marriage and fulfilling our shared dream of going into the food business. With a lot of work and bumps along the way, new paths began to open for us. One such path was the opportunity to venture into the ice cream business.

This adventure led to the writing of my book, *Beyond the Wall*, a book of stories, anecdotes, recipes, and values which explores the challenges that many Latino immigrants have overcome to reach our goals. *Beyond the Wall* shows the heart and hard work that was required to achieve our dream of conquering the American palate and its unique tastes.

Our ice cream shops began in a very modest and traditional way, but little by little, we started to conquer the whole world's taste and palate. I began to realize the great impact that David and I had created. People of all races, colors, and ethnicities visited our shops. David and I demonstrated a tremendous amount of creativity over that of our predecessors, and amid the difficult economic situations and limitations that befall new entrepreneurs, we gave rise to an impressive rainbow of flavors.

This experience caused me to consider the path that everyone travels before arriving in America. In every story you can see that it does not matter where you come from, what you don't have or how others label you. Everything is possible when there is true focus and a dream in the heart. In the book *Beyond the Wall*, you can find the fundamental advice that many have already applied and have helped us achieve our dreams. It's all about never giving up...and getting better every day.

REFLECTION

1. How has your family influenced your work ethic? Your career?

2. What is the greatest forgiveness that has ever been shown to you?

3. What do you do to get better every day?

BIOGRAPHY

Lupita Tovar, along with her husband David Castelan, are Mexican business owners who specialize in the art of Hispanic cuisine. Lupita was born in Villanueva, Zacatecas, where she opened her first business at the age of 19.

In America, Lupita and David have been able to win over the various palates of diners who visit their restaurants, filling their 20-year career with satisfaction and joy. Inspired by her trials and tribulations as a business woman, Lupita wrote her first book, *Beyond the Wall*, which features the advice and guidance of those who have struggled for success and sacrificed at great lengths to attain their dreams. During the project, Lupita enlisted the talents of her daughter, Esmeralda Castelan, a writer, performer, and speaker who was able to infuse the passion and integrity needed to complete the project. At the young age of 18, Esmeralda translated and rewrote the amazing tales of every person featured in *Beyond the Wall* and hand in hand with her mother, she assisted in the interviews that immortalized these stories full of triumphs, failures, and personal favorite recipes.

Lupita Tovar
lupitacastelan@live.com
(630) 550-2416

Doris N. Ayala, PhD, MJ

"We don't ever reach perfection, but we can reach a level of self-love and self-confidence that allows us to contribute as much as we can."

My life has been a journey of many experiences that have created the multifaceted person I am today. My life as a twin was a blessing, for to share this special bond with my twin sister is unlike any other. As I traveled from one journey, or transition in life, to another, numerous significant events have made an important impact on me.

JOURNEY TO ADULTHOOD

After World War II, the island of Puerto Rico suffered a severe economic depression. Its inhabitants were caught up in trying to survive in the poverty-stricken island. It was the beginning of the industrial revolution, and the companies in the continental U.S. began recruiting heavily on the island, offering people employment opportunities. When my twin and I were six months old, my parents immigrated to Chicago from Puerto Rico along with our eldest sister, who was one year older than we were. I give my parents a lot of credit for courageously taking an immense step in leaving everyone and everything behind, boarding a war plane and establishing themselves in a foreign country with a completely different culture, language and climate. United with a common cause, my parents and extended family members established themselves in neighborhoods where they readily maintained a supportive living environment.

My early years in America were but a vague memory, but not unpleasant. The family was always around and as children, we were a quiet group that didn't interrupt the adults. Instead, we were often left to ourselves to play. To be that young, innocent of life's tragedies, and ignorant of emotional pain, was wonderful. Yet, tragedy struck us all and I became cynical in my view of life itself. It was something that shaped my life forever. When I was seven years old, my secure world was thrown into upheaval when the unexpected happened—my mother was diagnosed with a brain tumor and died. The sudden loss jolted me and sent me into one of the most traumatic periods of my life.

I didn't understand the dynamics of her illness, yet when she died, it was then that I felt the full force of her not being there anymore. I was plunged into a dark world of helplessness, hopelessness, depression, bitterness, and anger. I remember hiding in the closets or bathrooms to cry, but nobody ever asked me about it or explored my pain. I was numb most of the time. For a long time, I emotionally detached myself from many people, including my family, and I wasn't in tune to how my sisters were feeling or experiencing the changes. It was years later that we began to share our loss and our pain. My father, bless his heart, worked hard to keep us fed and clothed, but didn't fully comprehend the depth of my loss.

In second grade, I decided I wasn't going to allow anyone to bully me or my twin. One day, when a peer pushed my sister out of the line we formed, I pushed her back and knew that my life would never be the same again. My grief had turned into anger.

Every year thereafter, my father was called up to school because I was involved in a fight, but my mission was accomplished because the other students, peers, and adults who disrespected me no longer pushed me around.

I was involved in fights until my freshman year in high school. Then one day I got into a fight with a friend who had joined a gang, and I became wary of the potential consequences of continuing to fight. I began thinking to myself that it was perhaps time to stop fighting, and instead be in control of something good, rather than the terrible acts of gang members. I began to question my purpose, who I was, and what I could do to make a difference in the world. I focused my efforts on my education and extracurricular activities – playing the violin and participating in the student council. But I had lost too many years being distracted in school. I did poorly, and when I was in my junior year, my counselor asked me what I wanted to study after high school. I said I wanted to be a doctor. I wanted to learn to heal people from disease and death. He looked at me and stated that I could only be a secretary and that was if I took my secretarial courses seriously. My heart dropped, but I vowed I would teach him a lesson, which later became my mission. During my senior year, I set upon a quest to become a doctor.

Since I was determined to go into the medical field, I decided to start as a nurse since my father was unable to afford medical school for me. I worked diligently and went to two years of community college where I took all my sciences and focused my efforts towards being accepted into a 4-year university. At last, I was accepted into the Loyola University School of Nursing.

JOURNEY OF THE MIND

With feelings of great pride, I started my year there. I was the only Latina. I had no friends or academic support. I felt alone, sad and unfocused. I sensed that I didn't belong there and felt emotionally exhausted. I knew I was navigating through a challenging situation, which changed my perspective on what I needed to do.

Meanwhile, my twin sister was enrolled at the UPR (University of Puerto Rico). I decided to return as well and I applied to the school of nursing at the medical center. Unfortunately, though, my transcripts never arrived, and I missed the enrollment period.

While in Puerto Rico, however, I met my husband, married and had four beautiful children. This delayed my academic pursuits, but I continued to persevere in pursuing my education. I decided to attend the nearby university and chose psychology as my major. However, there was a recession at the time and we weren't doing well in Puerto Rico. So, we decided to move the family to Chicago. I transferred to Northeastern Illinois

University (NEIU) and completed my bachelor's degree in psychology.

Afterward, I could not find a job with my degree, but I ended up finding employment as a social worker. Then in 1984, I received a full tuition scholarship to the University of Chicago and I began working towards a master's degree in social work. With four kids to raise and high academic expectations to meet, I knew that I had to focus all my efforts to survive this challenge. Unfortunately, my marriage was already a shambles. My husband saw my lifelong pursuit of my academic interests as a threat to our relationship and we decided we wouldn't make it together. We decided to divorce. I was left to struggle by myself with few resources. I had very little support from him to help with the children, but I was eager to move on with my newly found freedom. For years, my twin sister was my greatest source of support.

Then something illuminating happened that helped me conquer the sadness I carried deep within me. While doing my medical social work internship, I worked with a woman who had cancer. She had little time to live and her children were going to be orphaned. My work with them became a cathartic experience. As I experienced her pain and that of her children as they faced a future without their mother, I was able to understand my past encounter with my mother's death. It was a powerful experience as I realized I had freed myself from an unhappy past that I hadn't completely understood until that point in time.

I became a more integrated woman in so many ways

(mentally, emotionally, spiritually, intellectually) and I cultivated my musical interest in playing the piano and the violin. Additionally, I invested time in learning to protect myself through martial arts and firearms training. I knew I wanted to know how to defend myself and my loved ones against the widespread, common violence in our world.

My series of academic pursuits helped to reinforce my belief in myself and the potential for achieving success, whether it was working to get enough to feed and clothe my children, or obtaining the knowledge and skills needed to address the social problems of the communities where I worked.

My ongoing academic quests were important as I realized that education was key to a formative future. I relentlessly continued to find fulfillment by acquiring knowledge and skills with the end goal of being secure and mentally healthy. I also wanted to facilitate change in the lives of those who seek my professional services. Throughout these years, I completed courses and received certifications in marital and family therapy, Reiki, hypnosis, and biofeedback. I obtained my doctorate in clinical social work and a master's degree in jurisprudence in child and family law.

JOURNEY OF THE SOUL

I firmly believe that psychological and spiritual awareness are essential aspects to finding stability and happiness in life, and I wanted to experience spiritual enlightenment. After the tragic loss of my mother, I couldn't reconcile my faith in the Catholic religion. For years, I searched for a meaningful way to address my spiritual restlessness. Then I heard about the Q'ero shamans and went to Peru to attend a program with them. There I received the nine initiation rights of the shaman, which included the teachings and healing practices that would continue to inspire my spiritual mission. It was a powerfully transformative psychological and spiritual experience. I felt clear, centered, grounded and ready to embark on my next journey.

When I met my second partner in 1992, we entered into a synergistic relationship and developed a powerful alliance of mutual passion, intimacy, and commitment. Although we aren't compatible in cultural or religious ideals, we strive to overcome the barriers that affect our bond. Together, we became co-producers of mental health services to the Latino community through the Latino Family Institute. We have also launched numerous projects that focus on mental health issues.

Thus, through the struggles in my life, I was able to learn to be positive and efficacious with my time and efforts, to work with others and help them discover their own greatness to lead happier lives. I continue to experience the journey of my life in inspiring and challenging ways that enrich and enlighten me on a daily basis. As I experience my life, it unfolds, offering me exciting and fulfilling opportunities. I thank God for these countless blessings. I celebrate what I have become and am becoming as I explore how I can boost myself forward into the next stage of my journey.

My work with the many individuals that either have touched my life through professional alliances or through healing sessions, has been powerful. I view challenges as opportunities for growth and rather than resisting them, I embrace them and thank God for the lessons they teach. I have become accomplished in many areas of my life and share my knowledge and skills with those that I see in psychotherapy and my life in general. I firmly believe that we don't ever reach perfection, but we can reach a level of self-love and self-confidence that allows us to contribute as much as we can at a local, national, and global level.

REFLECTION

1. As your life unfolds, how do you evolve psychologically and spiritually to reach your goals?

2. How do you share your wisdom with others?

3. What stage are you in your life and how can you continue to develop your strengths to feel more grounded?

BIOGRAPHY

Doris N. Ayala, PhD, MJ was born Doris Nilsa in Arecibo, Puerto Rico. She has lived in Chicago and Puerto Rico during her lifetime. She has four amazing children and five precious grandchildren that provide the joyful medium of her existence.

Doris has been an entrepreneur of a number of businesses. She is the co-founder and executive director of the Latino Family Institute, which she still manages as she provides educational and mental health services to Latino and the community at large. She founded Sweeping Dimensions, a cleaning company whose mission was to employ single mothers with flexible hours and opportunities for growth. Her eldest daughter, Lariza Diaz, is now its successful proprietor. Dr. Ayala is also CEO of Clinical Dimensions, a company whose mission is to provide mental health services to children, adolescents, and adults. Her most recent company is Divorce Dimensions, which combines her knowledge and skills to facilitate pro se divorce to couples that wish to terminate their marriage.

Doris N. Ayala, PhD, MJ
dna@doctor-ayala.com
(708) 613-6063

Linda E. Alberty

"It is only after we account for the internal and external barriers limiting us that we can have the power to cultivate our excellent story."

Three things have remained constant in my life, forever fixed since childhood: God's faithfulness, my parent's support, and a moving truck. I learned early on how to quickly adapt in the face of extreme change. I grew up as a military dependent and have lived in 30 places in my life, attended eight elementary schools, and three high schools. Through it all, the love and honor I hold for my parents strengthened thanks to their sacrifices. They provided the best possible quality of life for me and my two sisters; they gave us much more than they ever had.

ARMY LIFE AND DIVERSITY

Army values, discipline, and respect guided me as a child. As much as they tried, my parents just could not get along. Many times, we dotted the map, joining my dad in military housing for a short time, only to return to a different "house" in Chicago because of my parent's incompatibility. I never knew how long we would stay or if another move was planned. I learned incredible moving skills, and to this day, I can pack an entire single-family home in less than 48 hours.

As a little girl, I could be found crying with great anguish, and sometimes demanding that the movers put my stuff down, for each move meant I had to make new friends in a world before social media. I greatly cherish the ability to assimilate to my environment and adapt to anyone, anywhere, at any time.

Despite the instability of my parent's love towards each other, separating and returning repeatedly to try to work it out, I persevered. I learned to trust in the love that never fails: God's love. I rested in His peace, and just when I thought I couldn't find my way, He remained there with me. With all the moving, however, I always had this intense, deep desire for a "home." In many ways, my faith in God provided stability for me, even though at times I attended one school for just a few months. When my parents were getting along and my family awaited new orders, we temporarily stayed on post at the guest house.

Whenever my father went on duty tours where we could not join him, we called the Chicagoland area our home base. I took great pride in sharing with my civilian classmates that my father was a U.S. Army Airborne Infantry Paratrooper. Other times, while attending schools on military bases, I would survey my classmates with delight, seeing a colorful rainbow of diversity. It is what I had come to expect. In third grade, while living in Italy, my classmates came from all over the world.

It was a shock whenever I attended civilian schools in the

U.S. and did not see diversity. I never saw the color of one's skin, where they were born, their gender, race, or economic class to be a barrier or a classifier. In fact, I never knew glass ceilings existed within structures of society until I got older and had to confront it head on. I only saw possibilities guided by the voice of my parents who told me I could accomplish anything I wanted with God on my side. Early exposure to so much diversity and constant change has allowed me to embrace being a diversity change agent today.

HEALING THROUGH PERSONAL FAITH

"But he said to me, 'My grace is sufficient for you, for my power is made perfect in weakness.' Therefore, I will boast all the more gladly about my weaknesses, so that Christ's power may rest on me." (2 Cor. 12:9)

When I was seven years old, my family was in a terrible car accident, leaving my father and me with life-threatening injuries. We survived, and sometimes I wonder if that is why our bond is so strong. The exact details of the accident have almost all been erased from my mind. A traumatic brain injury left me in a coma for six days. Uncertain of my future, the doctors made early predictions that I would remain in a vegetative state for the rest of my life. God had different plans. Imagine at just seven years old having to restart your life all over again—relearning all the basic things: how to move, walk, eat, speak, and even read. Though only a child, I fought to overcome the biggest setback of my life.

After the accident, it took eight months to reach a stable recovery. As I grew older, I gained a strong resiliency that helped me face my physical challenges. Whenever I experienced a vicious episode of migraines, I decided not to let it make me feel sorry for myself. Instead, I took proactive steps to deal with the situation: decreasing light and noise, and resting in a quiet place of solitude. I did whatever it took to finish my studies or commitments later, sometimes even waking up extra early before school to study or do my chores. I knew I could become better at my communication skills by reading, so I got my hands on every book I could read. I took personal responsibility, practicing my speech each day. I refused to let myself feel stigmatized or viewed as different by other kids.

My mother emphasized the importance of education and told me to reach for the stars. She had seen God's healing hand on my life. I have defied every statistic, and I work hard to ensure that others around me do the same. It is only after we account for the internal and external barriers limiting us that we can have the power to cultivate our excellent story...

Learning to cope with so many changes at such a young age is what made me mature so early in life. As a youth, I was 12 going on 21, and made a personal decision to surrender my life to Christ. I learned my identity as a daughter of the Most High. In my quest to build the roots I always desired, I got deeply involved with my church community, leading worship in the youth band, singing in the choir, and serving in the children's ministry. My mom sometimes worked nights, so if I did not have a way to get to church, I would save up my allowance from the week before and consider my options for a ride: call a taxi, ask my 90-year old neighbor, or call upon a church family. I was determined to get there, even if it meant being dropped off three hours before service. For me, this devotion to my faith was the first step in achieving a sense of "home" in my own life, even if I didn't know it yet.

CREATING LOCAL CHANGE IN A GLOBAL WORLD

On the morning of 9/11, I knew instantly that my life would never be the same. Officially stationed at Fort Campbell, Kentucky, both my parents were deployed—my mother to Operation Enduring Freedom-Afghanistan and my father to Operation Iraqi Freedom. To finish the year at Fort Campbell, a blue ribbon high school, our family readiness plan directed me to stay with my dad's first sergeant's wife, Ms. Lani. She embraced me as her own daughter, and even today still showers me with love and kindness. But receiving a letter from my parents during their deployment was my sweetest relief, reminding me that "home" is more than a place. I held on to my faith in God and their love for me.

Ultimately, that connection to a feeling of "home" guided me to one of the greatest gifts in life. A few years back, some new friends and I were talking about something we always wanted to do. I finally voiced my own secret dream, "I've always wanted to go to downtown Chicago on Christmas morning and love on the homeless with food and blankets, but I don't have anyone that would do it with me." Suddenly, someone replied, "I'll go with you." "Yea, me too," said another. What a surprise! Within five minutes, Operation Jesus was being assembled right before me.

Now, several years later, it has grown to include hundreds of volunteers, donors, corporate partnerships, and a renewed sense of "home." Through a simple dream, grounded in a promise of God's love and my parent's constant support, I have created something that brings a feeling of "home" to so many who lack a literal home. And the best part is it isn't just about me doing the work. I am connecting people across cities, states, and even countries.

WORKING TOWARDS EXCELLENCE

Because I constantly moved in my childhood and all throughout my high school years, I made sure to make college impactful by building friendships and investing quality time with my student campus ministry. I became the first in my family to graduate from a four-year university. I took 16 credit hours, worked two jobs, and had to meet strict physical standards as an Air Force ROTC cadet. Required to attend physical training at 6 a.m. three times a week, I accepted commitments and remembered the call on my life. For me, education acted as the key to create my future, providing me a place in the world.

At 21, I decided to stay in school to pursue my master's degree, with great personal sacrifices. I condensed a two-year graduate program into one, while working close to full-time. During graduate school, I spent whatever evenings and weekends I had helping families in the area with their résumés in exchange for a home-cooked meal. This reminded me that in life it takes a village to provide that sense of "home" we all long for.

I continued to help people with their résumés even after I graduated and accepted my first full-time position as Assistant Director for Alumni Relations at Northern Illinois University. I easily helped hundreds of individuals and families prepare for their future, never keeping count or recognizing the impact I was having on them but knowing deep inside that we were part of one global family. Over the next few years, I received countless messages thanking me and informing me of career advancements, including promotions, raises, and new jobs. This encouraged me to consider becoming a business owner and carry on my tradition of helping people beyond simply preparing their résumé.

Nine years later, I said goodbye to a corporate career and launched my professional consulting firm, CULTIVATE EXCELLENCE, as a full-time entrepreneur. I founded it on the story of Daniel in the Bible. "Then this Daniel was preferred above the presidents and princes, because an excellent spirit was in him; and the king thought to set him over the whole realm." (Daniel 6:3).

I am who I am today by the grace of God. Everything I have comes to me because of Him. I have had my ups and downs. I have been raw, vulnerable, and most importantly, I have learned to sit with my pain to overcome and destroy the things that used to hold me back: the constant life seemingly without "home", the lonely leader syndrome, feeling the sting and void of motherhood, recognizing and disarming unhealthy relationships with destructive cycles, and learning more about myself. Every day, God's mercy heals, restores, and creates me anew in my own excellence.

I rejoice today. I am on a path towards becoming healthy and whole in every way, having found "home" within me, gifted by God. I love to empower others with practical solutions that awaken the excellence that lies within. Thus, my business is growing. My personal life is thriving and I have been blessed with the most patient and kind love. I call him my sweetheart and he calls me his darling. I look forward to whatever lays ahead.

REFLECTION

1. Have you ever found yourself trying to escape the present and/or past by living in the future?

2. What role does faith have in your journey as you overcome personal and professional setbacks?

3. How are you accounting for the barriers that have limited you as you cultivate your own story of excellence?

BIOGRAPHY

Linda E. Alberty combines her understanding of the public and private sectors with expertise in integrated marketing communications, brand-building, and career empowerment to provide the ultimate value to those she serves. As president and founder of CULTIVATE EXCELLENCE Consulting, Linda partners with hundreds of individuals and organizations to rewrite their personal and professional stories and help clients reach the next level by cultivating the excellence that lies within.

Linda continually strives to cultivate strategic and mutually beneficial partnerships that foster collaboration, leadership, and innovation. Appointed by the Mayor of Lisle to serve on the Village's Economic Development Commission, Linda lends her expertise in marketing to promote the Village's economic vitality. She also serves on New Skills for Youth (NSFY), a cross-sector team mandated by The Illinois State Board of Education. As a well-known blogger and sought after motivational speaker, Linda is also a 2016 recipient of the Influential Women in Business Award from the Daily Herald Business Ledger.

Linda holds an M.A. in Communication from Northern Illinois University. She is also founder of Operation Jesus, a volunteer organization that provides food, clothing and care for the homeless, and a proud graduate of The United Neighborhood Organization's (UNO) Corporate Leadership Institute.

Linda E. Alberty
linda@cultivateexcellence.com
www.cultivateexcellence.com
(815) 200-6892

Irma Siboney González

"Every situation brings you the opportunity to heal,
grow and release."

Ever since I can remember, I've felt special, different, just as each of you is unique. In my case, I started the search for my life mission at a very early age, because it is said that there are two important moments in life: the day we are born and the day we discover our purpose.

There have been many moments that have left a mark on my life. These moments are what make us different and create the challenges that we must overcome to forge our current personalities. In my case, the first transcendental, crucial moment in my life was my near-death experience. I had heard that at such a time your whole life flashes before you in seconds, like a movie, when you're on the brink of death, but I had always considered it part of the fantasies that we use to explain the unknown. However, now I can say that I lived it.

THE AWAKENING

At the age of 22, I faced a life-and-death struggle with a strong bout of peritonitis. The doctors were in shock because I was not diagnosed upon arrival at the hospital. At that time, I experienced frequent fits of colitis and chronic gastritis, so my visit did not appear out of the ordinary. After spending all night anesthetized and not improving or worsening, I was finally taken into the ER, where my life flashed before my eyes. I had not lived a bad life; on the contrary, I was a very restless, mischievous little girl who questioned everything that existed, yet was very religious and family-oriented. I went through many struggles before high school, but then I had several important achievements for a girl my age.

In high school, I was homecoming queen, acted in diverse plays, overcame the bullying of the past, made new friends and was able to forge my self-esteem as I overcame obstacles and challenges. Yet, I still felt that I had not lived fully or knew what it really meant to live fully, although I had definitely lived the best I could. I had a calm conscience, having tried to give the best of myself always. However, there comes that special moment where you visualize your life from an outside perspective, and you are sincere with yourself and that divine essence, and you ask for another opportunity.

Thus began a very special connection which I did not notice at first. My life seemed to continue normally. I asked to be able to love my surroundings intensely, know the world better and enjoy the family, which I began to do. I was able to appreciate the university, act in plays, assist in workshops like television, radio, contemporary dance, and perform in works of theatre. I participated in workshops where I learned to do the things I was passionate about. I was also able to travel as I had always wanted to do.

THE DISCOVERY

I earned a diploma in English in England where I studied for seven months on an exchange program. I got to know much of Europe and learned various customs, traditions, arts, and tastes. I traveled by train, but it was quite a challenge and sometimes I went without eating or lodging for the night. I stayed in airports or train stations. I started to understand life more, because I also realized that everywhere in the world, even in the worst circumstances, there will always be good people who look out for others and help you.

I thanked God for letting me experience hunger and cold. I felt more alive and I valued my country, people, family, and home more than ever before. I believe sometimes we need to isolate ourselves and live without in order to enjoy abundance. It was an experience that opened my eyes and my faith in the love that exists, the love that people have for each other. I analyzed how every circumstance in which a person finds themselves- -the country, social, cultural, and religious rules-- molds a person's personality and perspective. How beautiful it is to share customs and cultures. I made many long-lasting friendships.

I returned to Mexico and wanted to continue learning. A career in business is so broad that it allows you to know a little about everything. I received an honorable mention and earned a diploma in international business from Peking University, getting to know yet another completely different culture. I had the opportunity to visit Shanghai, Hong Kong, and Thailand and learned a lot from those cultures.

In 2006, while in Thailand, I visited Phuket Island, which had suffered a terrible tsunami in 2004. It made me meditate about how things can be rebuilt after being completely destroyed, like a phoenix rising from the ashes, but only if your spirit has not been broken.

Traveling alone made me lose fear. I discovered that every situation brings you the opportunity to heal, grow and release. It is beautiful to face your fears and enjoy the presence of yourself. Being so far away, in my solitude, I found the greatest strength in knowing that I could count on myself and do what I wanted to do, when I wanted to live and give. It does not matter what country you're in; you will always receive, according to the law of attraction and correspondence.

THE SEARCH

Trying to find the balance between working, following my passion, and continuing to learn, I started working in family-owned companies and studying for a master's degree in innovation and development. I tried to apply all my knowledge. I started work as a consultant and decided to give dance classes to girls and adolescents in a cultural center, moving between cities to share my experiences and abilities as much as possible. I graduated from my master's program with honors and I thought that I had everything, but I remained restless.

Then I suddenly experienced changes in my life that left me feeling shaken. I discovered reiki as a bridge to find inner peace and a deep connection with God. I started a new life challenge, attempting to live in love, without judgment, and following these basic principles:

1. Just for today, do not worry.

2. Just for today, do not get angry.

3. Just for today, be kind to all those around you and respect every living being.

4. Just for today, do your work honestly.

5. Just for today, be thankful for all the blessings in your life.

These principles helped me realize why I cannot judge what I do not understand. We live in a world that is imperfect and within the imperfect, we are in the perfect moment, in the perfect circumstance that at that moment you need for your evolution. I meet different mentors who teach me that our being will always be anxious and hungry for knowledge and we will seek balance in our life. We have to be who we were born to be.

I discovered that by sending out vibrations, I could use my gifts and talents for others. There is nothing to fear, because things are sown, and I will not harvest too quickly. Success is like Japanese bamboo: the first few months, nothing substantial occurs. Even in the first seven years, nothing happens because it is set to take root and have a solid base. But in the seventh year, the bamboo plant can grow to more than 30 meters in a period of six weeks. Success is something that is still being built, but does not come easily.

I, like you, am a woman who struggles every day to get ahead and feel successful because I came to this country to try to prove myself. That's why we are successful, because we decided to leave our comfort zone and move to the country of the great challenges. It has not been easy. Even as a professional with a valid license in this country, I am undocumented and without legal status, just like any other woman who has fought and who has to demonstrate with work what really matters. Titles or degrees don't matter; you can only count on the resources you have within yourself to be successful.

Nonetheless, I've had great satisfaction. I've been involved in some organizations and foundations that led me to media communications with an internet radio and television program. The holistic show gives the community more tools than I ever had, and it has changed my life. I'm writing a book in which I discuss my life discoveries, and the experiences that have helped me connect with my being.

THE CHALLENGE

I try to live my passion and use my knowledge and abilities because this country has taught me that if we do not persist and persevere, the world will eat us up. We are here to rule the world-- not the other way around--and even if we do not see the immediate opportunities, if we focus our faith, passion, and love, the doors will open for us in time. I feel I'm at the best moment of my life, and I enjoy spending my time between working and advancing my career in a growing company, being a dancer (which is my passion), being a conduit in the world with my work, therapies, and the Holistic Life channel, and giving workshops on empowerment and overcoming your environment.

However, I feel frustrated in this country, like many professional people who want to contribute, but whose legal status prevents them from doing so. How is it possible that people who come to this country with the hope of making a better world, wanting to reach a better future, looking for a better society and trying to make America a better place, are regarded as cogs in a machine. We have put our heart, our effort, our hope into this country, trying to offer our best talents, abilities, and knowledge. We are just like our ancestors before us who came to this country and succeeded in making it a better place.

I ask myself as a professional person, a worker, and a human, what I can do to change this situation. I do not know if I have lived a lot or a little. I only know that I have tried to live to the fullest every day of my life. I am a woman who has fallen many times. But every time I've fallen, I've thanked God, because I feel more human, and it's getting easier to get up. I'm learning more, and I'm happier every day. That's why I am so happy to be in this moment, in this life.

I believe that as Latina women, we have much to contribute to this multicultural society, from our values, culture and life philosophies, to the experiences that have transformed us. This is what gives us a unique history, because I consider myself unique like you. You have much to contribute and much to share. You do not need to be on the verge of death, nor be the victim of a tragic situation to take control of your life and do a self-analysis. The time to transform yourself is today. I invite you to be the owner of your story, to be your own author. I hope my story helps you understand that you do not need to be on your deathbed to start living. The most precious thing we have in this life is time to do what you want to do.

REFLECTION

1. Have you ever felt more appreciative because you have gone without something?

2. What do you think your greatest contribution can be in a multicultural society?

3. What connection do you feel with those around you?

BIOGRAPHY

Siboney Gonzalez was born in Zacatecas and has a degree in business administration, a certificate in international business and a master's degree in innovation and development, all from the Monterrey Institute of Technology and Higher Education. She is a professional businesswoman with more than 15 years of experience handling various family businesses. She also has four years of experience in consulting, and five years in network marketing.

Siboney has worked in public accounting and has participated as a volunteer for several organizations, including Latin Women in Action and the Association of the Honduran Culture in Chicago. She has been a co-host of *Para Ti y Todo* Chicago, an online television show, and participated in another called *Historias Bajo la Luna*. She has served as emcee at various events in Chicago and given personal development workshops to low-income women. She has studied alternative healing techniques such as Master Reiki, Theta healing, and Biodecodification.

Siboney also belly dances and teaches physical training, alternating various disciplines such as yoga, Pilates, Tae Bo, hip-hop, etc. She writes songs and is currently writing a book about self-improvement.

Her life philosophy is to keep learning and inspiring people to contribute in some way to humanity.

Irma Siboney González
lic.siboneygonzalez@gmail.com
+52(492)870-4514

Mariela G. Camacho-Kimble

"Failure is sometimes the universe telling you your mission in life is somewhere else."

My name is Mariela Camacho-Kimble and I was born in Guadalajara, Mexico. At the age of 17, I came to Chicago with the purpose of learning the English language. My family has always considered dedication and continuous improvement as the way to achieve success.

I was raised in a small town. My parents have owned a family corn husking business, Hojas El Chicano e Hijos Inc., for 30 years. They provide employment for many people in the community. It has been very difficult for them to keep the business open, but working together as a family, we have managed to keep it thriving. I had a beautiful childhood full of love from my family.

When I was six years old, my mother had to leave us with my father's family because she needed a kidney transplant. As a child, I was so confused as to why she left us with people that were like strangers. My brother, Jaime, was the one taking care of me at all times, hugging me when I was sad, playing with me, and protecting me from everything he could. I learned that there were lots of people that wanted to sabotage us, and would tell us that my mother wasn't coming back and that she was going to die. Those were the most stressful times of my childhood. I felt lost, confused, insecure, and very scared that what they were saying was true.

After 18 months, my mother came back home, but nothing was ever the same. Most of the time, I was scared to lose my mother again. Since then, I have been taking care of my mother as her disease progresses. This experience from my childhood taught me to appreciate and love my parents.

A NEW LIFE

At the age of 19, I married a man who was 10 years older than me. Like many other women, I took my vows thinking that he was going to be my husband for the rest of my life. But it did not work out that way. His controlling ways and manipulation tore me down and made me very insecure. I had a very controlling father when I was a child and I found those same qualities comfortable in the man I took as my husband. Instead of feeling in love and free, I was treated like a little girl. I could not do anything without his consent. I felt trapped for many years. I was angry all the time and people misinterpreted it as me feeling superior over them. On the contrary, I was feeling lonelier than I had ever felt in my life.

During this difficult time, I focused all my energy into

my studies. I started taking English classes for almost two years before I started college classes. I was focused on obtaining my bachelor's degree in Nursing. After four years of marriage, everything started getting worse.

He was working most of the time, and I was focusing on myself. We started talking about divorce around July 2009. Two months later, I found out that I was five weeks pregnant. So, we continued living together as two strangers. When I was seven months along, he told me that he did not love me anymore. I thought that my world was ending. I did not know how I was going to survive by myself with a baby as a single mother. I felt lost, confused, and was in lots of mental and physical pain. I was studying more than ever, because my baby needed me to be strong.

On April 19, 2010, I had my beautiful baby boy, Noah. He became more important to me than I can express with words. When I saw his small and innocent face, I realized how lucky I was that he was healthy. He has been my sunshine in the most dark and difficult times. He has brought me smiles and has given me the strength that I needed to survive.

I went through postpartum depression and I was about to start the divorce process. I took one day at a time. I always had the support of my family, especially my brother Jaime. But the strength came from within. I always talk to myself and try to understand what could help me to feel better every day. I started meditating, running, and surrounding myself with positive, old friends that were there for me during this difficult time. I am a big believer that God always sends us what we can handle and nothing more, so my faith and inner strength helped me to overcome this situation at a young age.

I started the divorce process when Noah was a few months old, after finding out that his father was cheating on me during the entire relationship. I felt like I didn't know what was going on around me. I felt that our entire relationship was a lie. I started understanding why he was always working, and why I was always alone.

Getting divorced was one of the most challenging periods of my life. I was still very emotional and hurt by all the gossiping people around me. In those moments, I discovered my true friends and I will never forget who was with me during the whole process. The divorce was stressful, difficult, confusing, sad, maddening, but at the same time, it was an eye-opener. Sometimes I would question myself, wondering if I was doing the right thing, or if it would have been better to stay with him because we had a baby. I believe that most women go through this thoughtful moment. But in the end, I believe that kids are happier in a positive environment, full of love.

I let my lawyer do everything to protect my son in all possible ways. Someone told me that I had to see the divorce paper as the most valuable written paper in the world for my son. Now I cannot agree more with that statement. My brother Jaime was always with my son, making sure that we were doing well. The day I signed the divorce papers, my ex said, "We wouldn't be getting divorced if you did everything I told you to do." Right there I realized that I had made the best decision of my life.

Being a single mother has been challenging, but it has taught me many lessons. One lesson is that failure is part of life, and even the most successful people in the world have failed at some point. Always believe in yourself, listen to your inner voice, and never let anyone control you in any way.

THE TRAGEDY

The second year after my divorce, when I had about eight months left to finish nursing school, my brother had a car accident and died 14 days later. The pain of losing my cheerleader, best friend, and business partner was devastating and unbearable. My heart and soul hurt. The entire family has been devastated since Jaime's death. I have been in denial for the past three years, thinking that he is still alive and living in Mexico. Reminiscing about the love and loss makes me feel angry and extremely sad. All these feelings have stopped me from recovering and continuing to live the happy life I once did.

October 14, 2016 was the third anniversary of my brother's death. I decided to go to Mexico and face the reality of his absence by visiting his grave. I felt the same pain that I did at his funeral, but I knew that it was time to accept that he is no longer with me. I needed to face my biggest fear in order to find myself again and start giving all my positive energy to the people around me.

I have learned that the pain of losing a loved one never diminishes; we only learn to function within that grief. It doesn't matter how long it takes you to face your fears as long as you recognize that one day, you will have to do it.

Through it all, my mother has been, and continues to be, my true hero. She is the strongest woman I know. Her faith in God and inner strength has kept her alive these many years, battling her difficult disease. She is the person that made me who I am now. She did not agree with many decisions that I made in the past, but she has always been by my side, supporting me, loving me. My mother now is a little older, and her eyes show a deep emotional pain since my brother passed, but she still finds strength to dance in the rain.

The first year after Jaime's death, I continued with my life but was completely numb. I couldn't invest myself completely in anything. I suffered through nursing school, and eventually withdrew myself. The hospital was such a difficult place for me to be in my grief and I didn't want to be there. I am a believer that if you cannot give 100 percent in what you do, it is better not to do it.

Last time I was at the hospital doing my clinical hours, my patient died with orders not to resuscitate. I had to get him ready for the family before putting him in a bag. After that happened, I had nightmares for three months that I was putting my brother in that bag. Those were the worst nightmares that I have ever experienced. Then I made the decision to change careers and when I did, it was one of the hardest decisions of my life. For ten years I had studied to become a nurse and then didn't finish. I continued working on the project I started with my brother, which was importing corn husks for my parent's business while going to school. After intensive research, I found a way that I could transfer credits from nursing to a new career in health service management. In June of 2016, I graduated with honors with a bachelor's degree in Health Service Management and a 4.0 GPA. This experience helped me to accept my destiny.

GUIDED BY FAILURE

The quote that represents my life is from Jack Ma: "Never give up because you failed once or twice; know that failure is sometimes the universe telling you your mission in life is somewhere else." It is difficult to see failure as an experience and an opportunity for growth. Failing does not mean that you are a failure; it means that you are meant to be somewhere else in your life. Failing allows you to make a bigger impact elsewhere. The universe will always guide you and place you where you need to be.

I am now blessed with a beautiful family. My new husband has taught me true love by accepting who I am, supporting my dreams and holding my hand at difficult times. Together, we brought a beautiful little girl into this world. I now have two wonderful children that teach me how to be their mother, and help me see the positive side of life with their innocent and amazing smiles.

I started dreaming again, and started a new project that will allow me to help low income families in Mexico. I am launching my new business, PACHAMAMA Imports, Inc. I import handmade crafts such as décor, tableware, clothes, shoes, art, jewelry, etc. My goal is to share the beauty of Mexico, enriching the lives of both producers and purchasers. It is amazing to have the opportunity to share my roots with this project. Remember to believe in yourself, listen to your inner voice, and never stop dreaming. Never give up because you failed once or twice; get up and try again.

REFLECTION

1. How have you shown appreciation to the people around you that have supported you through difficult times?

2. How have you overcome your failures and turned them into opportunities?

3. When are you making your dreams come true?

BIOGRAPHY

Mariela G. Camacho-Kimble was born in Guadalajara, Mexico. She moved to the U.S. at the age of 17, unable to speak English. At a young age, she started taking care of her ill mother. This experience motivated her to pursue a degree in the healthcare area in order to improve services for her Hispanic community.

In 2011, she found herself a divorced, single mother without a well-paying job. She began managing her family business, Hojas El Chicano e Hijos Inc., with her brother while studying for her bachelor's degree. In 2013, she experienced the tragic loss of her brother, who was also her best friend and business partner, in a car accident. This tragedy changed her life completely.

In 2015, Mariela got remarried to an amazing man who embraces her dreams. They are raising two wonderful children, and family is her greatest blessing. Mariela's persistence brought her to where she is today: a bilingual business owner of PACHAMAMA Imports, Inc. with a bachelor's degree who is looking forward to making changes in healthcare and providing the best service possible. The goal of PACHAMAMA Imports is to share the beauty of Mexico and enrich the lives of both producers and purchasers.

Mariela Camacho-Kimble
mckpachamama@gmail.com
(312) 804-0822

Dolly Zea

"If you dream, dream big!"

I was born in Colombia in a very poor neighborhood. My economic situation was very desperate and even deplorable, but that did not stop me from dreaming big and thinking that someday soon my circumstances would change! And little by little, my hopes, illusions, and dreams came true. It took a lot of effort and sacrifices, but it happened. Everything I dreamt about yesterday, has come true today!

BORN FOR BUSINESS

I have been working since I was eight years old because that is when I had the opportunity to enter the business world. I had a mini-company that sold candies at the corner of the street by the stoplights to help my sick mother, who taught me so many values and mentored me through life. She told me that even through adversity we should think positively no matter how difficult life became. We needed to have tenacity and make a concerted effort to overcome the obstacles that life sends our way.

As the years went by, I continued to work and study. I worked odd jobs to pay my bills and during the day I worked at a private school. When I was in high school, I started to work during the day and attend school at night. In my country, it is common for someone to work and study at night. This allowed me to put myself through the university to study business administration.

At the age of 18, I was fortunate enough to start businesses while working for my employer. I realized that my passion was to help my community and so I became an employer, offering members of the community a source of income. At one point, I had around 200 employees under my supervision. I imported products and kept my business going no matter what happened. For example, one time, we were notified that there was going to be an electric power outage. We did not have electricity from 7 a.m. to 9 a.m.

Shortly after that experience, I read in a newspaper that there was an electric generator for sale. I decided to buy it, then contracted a secretary, rented an office and hired an electrician. I had a virtual inventory. I also got a few of the catalogs from electric generators and learned all about them. From there I was able to train my clients on how to use the generators. Then corporations began to hire me to train their employees as well. I became the owner of this incredible business. I used the newspapers to advertise my company with two different types of advertisements: one stating that I bought electric generators and another one saying I sold electric generators for all kind of businesses.

My goal was to serve the needs of hotels, homes, restaurants and all people living in houses who were experiencing the periodic electrical problems and wanted a solution. I invested people's capital intelligently to build a better company.

After that, I decided to open a textile business along the borders of Brazil, Panama, Venezuela, and Ecuador as well as some European countries. I started to travel, even to Spain where I bought blankets, and Italy where I bought rosaries and other religious items. I traveled all over and this is how I met the man of my dreams-- a visionary person, dreamer, and leader by nature. He was also a police investigator and high ranking official in Columbia.

BIG FAMILY DREAMS

Two years after our marriage, Colombia's economic situation was in decline so we immigrated to America. Five years later, in 2001, our first daughter was born. Like most immigrants that come here, at first we had to work in jobs that were not what we wanted. I was babysitting and my husband was working in a hotel maintenance department and delivering pizza as well.

As our daughter grew, we began making plans for her future and one of them was to have her attend Harvard University. As she grew older, this dream not only came true (she went to Harvard), but she also attended Stanford. She was the catalyst for us to always dream big!

When Julianna was three, I became pregnant with my second child, Jeimar, and he was born seven weeks premature. To this day he has complications caused by a condition named attention deficit hyperactivity disorder (ADHD). It is borderline autism, but his was severe, and his prognosis was bleak. Doctors said Jey would not be able to walk or ride a bike, he would always have speech problems and would not ever become an independent person. The future looked dark. As a solution, they offered medication combined with therapy.

I decided not to medicate him because there were too many adverse side effects to the drugs they suggested. Instead, we took him to all the therapies possible, along with all the courses and classes that were offered to give all the support he needed. Jey surpassed everyone's expectations. He has been a mini-businessman since age 11.

We taught him to develop short, medium, and long term goals. He bought his first computer with his own money that he earned walking dogs. He also created a flyer, distributed it in our neighborhood and now has a big clientele. Soon he will be going to Japan with 22 other children that were invited to take classes in a drawing technique called MANGA, which is a sort of cartoon strip. He takes classes in art, music, violin, guitar, karate and he is very disciplined and well trained.

To go to Japan, he obtained a permit from the city to play music in the metro and collected donations as he played his violin or guitar for people who passed by. As parents, we are filled with great pride that he is able to live each of his own experiences.

Our third son Sean is sweet, delicate, brilliant, and an innate leader. He is a great athlete and loves music as well. He is my pride, my love, my everything!

POSITIVE FORCES

My work experience here in the U. S. has been good and we have accomplished much. We were the pioneers in the satellite industry, working for Dish Network and Direct TV. We even received an award from the newspaper Hoy, for being the number one salesperson for Direct TV. We have won trips to Africa, the World Cup in Brazil, and the Super Bowl- all due to our dedication, vision, optimism, and most of all, the great effort and sacrifices we have put forth in everything!

I am in a happy marriage and my biggest and greatest force is my family. I'm a person that plays a big role daily within my family, and I'm always projecting new things. Now we are concentrating on this project called Miss Juventud. The program is for young Latinas with a goal of getting them involved, away from bad friends, and keeping them busy and productive. Like my grandmother used to say, idle hands are the devil's playground!

We need to work hard for Miss Juventud and make sure it has great teachers. We offer dance classes, modeling, make up, hair, dress, etc., but our true goal is to help the girls achieve higher education. We have taken 56 girls to Harvard University, MIT, and Princeton. It was an amazing tour with conferences and for many of the families, it was the first time they had ever left Chicago.

Miss Juventud has been very successful and serving the Hispanic community has been one of the best things we have ever done. I feel very proud of my roots and for all the things we can do through our families, our communities, and fellow Colombians.

Currently, I'm working on a project developed by Amway and have gotten many families involved to find financial and personal freedom. Thanks to this business, I travel a lot and dream that someday I can be financially free. Then there would be no limit to what I could accomplish helping others through various projects. That is what I want to do most: help make the dreams of Latinas come true, for the mothers, my friends, and all those who have planted a seed to make this country strong.

I'm very proud to be Colombian. No matter how difficult life gets wherever you are, there is always something good behind the bad times and there is always something good if you have faith to move mountains. If you dream, dream big!

REFLECTION

1. Are you dreaming big? Do you think you can accomplish your dreams?

2. What skills and resources do you need to achieve your goals?

3. Are you able to persevere when things get difficult?

BIOGRAPHY

Dolly Zea is a successful entrepreneur and native of Bogota, Columbia, where she received her education in business administration. She has always had a desire to support the needy and feels that the best way to solve unemployment is to become a source of employment as an entrepreneur. She entered the corporate world working for De Horizonte International, where she worked from 1992-98.

After marrying the love of her life, Jeimar Neiza, Dolly first experienced the U.S. on her honeymoon. The couple immigrated to the U.S. and eventually moved to Chicago where they launched Neizas Enterprise, a satellite retailer, which was honored in 2012 by the Chicago Tribune. In 2013 she was named the number one dealer of DirectTV for the Latin market in the U.S.

She currently manages the company Doctor Cell, and is an independent business woman of the Amway corporation in Canada, Columba and the U.S. as well as executive director of a Hispanic TV show, *Gente de Exito*. Dolly is also the founder of Miss Juventud, a program to help ayoung Latinas.

Dolly and her husband are raising three children and continuing to write their story in America, despite life's little obstacles.

Dolly Zea
missjuventud@yahoo.com
(773) 791-0966

KNOWING AND OWNING YOUR WORTH: THE IMPORTANCE OF AUTHENTICITY

Cynthia Gomez

"I believe it is in our authenticity that we are our most powerful and able to genuinely connect with others."

"*Tell me who your friends are and I'll tell you who you are*" and "*Darte Valor*", (meaning "give yourself value") were two expressions I often heard from my parents as I was growing up in the Washington Heights area of New York City. These words guided the choices I made and were core values instilled in me from childhood.

My mom told me it is important to love yourself, have compassion and know your worth. If you don't give yourself worth, no one else will. It wasn't until a few years ago that my parent's words really connected with me; I had to learn through experience.

I learned to choose friends who were goal-oriented, encouraging, and would not turn their backs on me. I am grateful to have a strong support network of family and friends to inspire me and who encourage each other to stretch beyond our comfort zones.

GOOD ENOUGH?

Since I was a child, my parents told me I am strong and can do whatever I want in life. They also taught me to be positive, kind, and giving. Hearing these words and living them are two different things.

In high school and college, it was hard to believe my parents because I would constantly compare myself to others. I would judge myself as not good or smart enough. I just didn't believe in my own worth, intelligence and value, or the contribution that I could make even when others saw it in me.

When I reached a milestone, I wanted to quickly move on to the next one because I felt it was not enough. I never savored the moment and celebrated my small victories. Instead, I became self-conscious of what others thought of me. I was so consumed with other's opinions that I did not acknowledge my individual growth as a woman. "*Darte valor*", or giving myself worth, didn't connect with me yet because I had a limiting belief that I was not good enough.

I grew up with limited resources, but my parents always believed in the value of education and wanted me to go to college. They believed it would open doors for me. So through financial sacrifice from family, I was able to attend local parochial schools in Washington Heights. I was a diligent student and took my homework very seriously.

After graduation, I wanted to remain close to home, but yearned to expand my knowledge, experience a new environment, and learn about new cultures. My choices were Fordham

University or St. John's University because I could commute to them from home. Then, during one of our guidance sessions, my counselor asked if I had heard of Barnard College, the women's college at Columbia University. She explained it was a great school and I had a good chance of getting in. Even though my GPA and test results were good enough, I didn't believe they would admit me. But I applied and was accepted, which was a huge accomplishment for me and my family.

I was part of the Higher Education Opportunity Program (HEOP) which provided guidance and financial support for transitioning to college. I was accepted to Fordham and St. John's too, but in my heart, I knew Barnard would be home. I was scared, because I had friends going to Fordham and St. John's and it felt more comfortable to follow them than to create my own path. However, I considered my parent's wise words through the years, decided to trust my intuition and accepted my admission to Barnard on the enrollment deadline day.

The transition was challenging, especially my first semester. It was a culture shock and an adjustment. I felt like I didn't belong. I had negative thoughts about not being good enough and at one point I even thought my admission was a mistake. I compared myself to others to "prove" I wasn't smart enough.

Career wise, I also didn't know what I wanted to do. I decided I should be something that sounded great to *others* - a doctor or a lawyer- since I didn't have any way to know that there were many other career possibilities for me, for what *I* would like. Eventually, I chose a liberal arts major. What was I going to do with that? Would I make any money? What would people think? I always knew that I wanted to help people, but I didn't know how. I also didn't believe I was worthy of making a contribution that way. The voice of insecurity had taken control of my mind.

My self-doubts during college definitely held me back. For example, I wouldn't ask questions for fear that my classmates would think I was unintelligent. I was worried I wouldn't be understood because of my accent, even though that never happened. Without recognizing it, I was dimming my true self and feeling different in every aspect of my life. I was slowly losing my essence as a genuinely joyous, loving, kind person.

Eventually, I found amazing and supportive counselors along my journey that saw my potential and encouraged me, guided me, and pushed me through my self-doubt. I worked hard and persevered, shutting the "not enough" conversations out of my head. I graduated from Barnard with a BA in Sociology and Political Science. But the bigger accomplishment was being the first in my family to graduate from a 4-year college. It was a great milestone for my Dominican born parents who worked hard so that I could receive an education and "make something out of myself."

I'm glad I followed my instinct to attend Barnard. It gave me an amazing education and I am proud to be an alum. In fact, I have gone back to mentor and I have a great support network of strong Barnard women who encourage and celebrate each other's accomplishments and endeavors.

WHAT I KNOW NOW

When I was growing up, I was afraid to speak up and say what was on my mind, especially at school. Now I've learned it's important to be your authentic self. It is the most freeing, and I believe it is in our authenticity that we are our most powerful and able to genuinely connect with others. It made me a stronger Latina woman.

Throughout life, I always try to be self-aware, support myself, improve, and work on my weaknesses. Therefore, I enjoy reading self-help books, such as *The Secret* by Rhonda Byrne. My biggest takeaway from the book was to be clear on my vision, believe that I can achieve it, and be grateful. I learned the importance of authentically giving what you want unconditionally in order to receive. This perspective gave me a new understanding of the life that I wanted to create for myself.

I didn't become a doctor or a lawyer, but my career started in business. I received my first internship through a professional development program, INROADS at Avon Products, Inc. in human resources. I learned valuable corporate skills and I was blessed with an amazing mentor who became a great friend and advisor. I'm grateful for this internship because it helped me build my resume with transferrable skills to help me land my first full-time opportunity at Citigroup after graduation. Two years later, I wanted to become more well-rounded and decided to pursue my Masters in Public Administration at Baruch College.

I realized that I had a connection to human resources because it involved several areas of interest to me, including business, helping people, and making an impact. That is what I wanted to do all along, but didn't know it then. I felt that my degree in Sociology and my experience in business would align. With this realization and soul searching, I decided to transition my career to the staffing industry at Robert Half International during the economic downturn of 2008. During this time, I learned persistence and the importance of being courageous. I was determined to succeed, so I worked hard and persevered.

I also wanted to move into a management opportunity to empower and develop a staff and I envisioned myself doing it. I shared my results and contributions with my supervisors and asked for my first management role. I worked hard, believed and trusted in myself, and soon I received *another* management role. When you know your worth and that you are a contributor, you ask for what you want.

I then transitioned to corporate recruitment in the entertainment industry at Warner Music Group and Home Box Office, Inc. I love what I do. In my work, I identify solid talent for the business and help professionals find the next step in their career. In connecting with who I am and the contributions that I make, I also realized that I also enjoy giving back to the community. Three friends and I created a nonprofit organization called "Fostering Leadership 4 Young Women" with the goal of supporting young women in foster care with professional and leadership development.

I have learned that patience is a virtue and things in life eventually fall into place. I'm grateful for my experiences in college because it made me stronger and I learned the importance of being authentic and knowing my worth. Now, whenever the "not enough" conversations arise, I remind myself that I'm unique with what I bring to the table, and I *do not* compare myself to others. If I encounter challenges, my approach is to persevere, know my value, have compassion for myself and not take things so seriously. I continue to learn, grow, and trust my life's journey and that my core values will support me with the choices I make. I also want to instill these values in my daughter for her future.

LESSONS FROM MY DAUGHTER

The birth of my daughter was a transformative moment for me. It was an experience that allowed me to put things into perspective. It goes back to knowing your worth, being authentic, and setting boundaries.

Now that I am a mother, my daughter is a reminder of my strength, the importance of being in the moment, being grateful, and most importantly, loving myself. Sharing the experience of motherhood with other women has allowed me to connect authentically on a level that was not possible before. The strength, difficulty, and reward of becoming a mother allowed me to love something greater than me. It's no longer important how I am in comparison to others. My priority is to be the best I can be for my daughter.

Gratitude and saying daily affirmations has helped me live in the moment, knowing and owning my worth and unique skills and talents that are a contribution to the world. One of my favorite inspiring quotes that I read often to remind myself about my contributions is from Marianne Williamson:

"Our deepest fear is not that we are inadequate. Our deepest fear is that we are powerful beyond measure. It is our light, not our darkness that most frightens us. We ask ourselves, who am I to be brilliant, gorgeous, talented, and fabulous? Actually, who are you not to be? You are a child of God. Playing small does not serve the world. There is nothing enlightened about shrinking so that other people won't feel insecure around you. We are all meant to shine, as children do. We were born to make manifest the glory of God that is within us. It's not just in some of us; it's in everyone. And as we let our own light shine, we unconsciously give other people permission to do the same. As we are liberated from our own fear, our presence automatically liberates others."

We all have unique contributions that we get to own and share with the world. The possibilities are endless! We can play small because of our internal self-doubt dialogues and limiting beliefs, or we can own and know our worth and surround ourselves with individuals that will support us to stretch beyond our comfort zones. *Darte Valor!*

REFLECTION

1. What are your limiting beliefs?

2. What are your core values and how have they impacted the choices you have made?

3. What is the impact and legacy that you dream to make in your community? Is it authentic to you?

BIOGRAPHY

Cynthia Gomez is a human resources professional with experience in the corporate recruitment and staffing industry. She is a Talent Acquisition Recruiter who is passionate about identifying, mentoring, and developing professionals.

Cynthia had a humble beginning, born and raised in the Washington Heights section of New York City. Her parents of Dominican heritage instilled in her the importance of education, commitment, and dedication. They taught her that education is the key to success and to always believe that dreams can be achieved. Through hard work and determination, she attended Barnard College at Columbia University for her undergraduate degree in Sociology and Political Science. Cynthia also holds a Master's in Public Administration from Baruch College.

Cynthia believes in empowerment through contribution. She is passionate about mentoring adults and teenagers in leadership development. She has supported young women with professional and leadership development as co-founder of Fostering Leadership for Young Women, Inc. She has also volunteered as a leadership development mentor at a life coaching and training organization.

Cynthia lives with her wonderful husband in Queens, New York and is a proud mother to her beautiful daughter, Sophia Joy.

Cynthia Gomez
2cynthia.gomez@gmail.com

Jeanette V. Miranda

"Being maternal comes from the heart and soul."

In December 2010, my husband Orlando and I arrived at our appointment in Bayamon, Puerto Rico to see Dr. Pedro Beauchamp. Accompanying us was our friend, Leticia. Dr. Beauchamp came highly recommended by my cousin, Amy. He was the first doctor to successfully perform IVF in Puerto Rico. After trying to get pregnant for eight years using various methods, and experiencing two failed IVF attempts, we were confident that God had put us here.

We had been on the island for several weeks preparing for this day. All the tests I had undergone revealed that my body was ready for the extraction of my eggs. The only thing left to do was for my husband to perform his part. Orlando was nervous, and I asked him if he needed my help. He assured me he would be fine on his own. We both laughed. We looked into each other eyes with so much love, knowing that our dream of having our own child would finally be realized! I waited patiently for Orlando for what seemed to be an eternity.

ARE WE ENOUGH

Finally, Orlando came into my room. Then the doctor walked in and we knew from the look on his face that something was wrong. He proceeded to inform us that Orlando's sperm count was zero. Therefore, there were no viable sperm to work with. All I wanted to do was run out of there, but I had to compose myself. We thanked the doctor and his great staff and went to the waiting area where Leticia was waiting for us. As we approached her, Leticia said out loud, "Wow, that was fast!" with excitement in her voice. I looked at her but I couldn't speak; words couldn't come out of my mouth. I was able to motion to her to exit.

Instead of taking the elevator, all three of us walked up several flights of stairs in silence. I was numb. As soon as we reached the car, Orlando and I started bawling. After all these years, we had come to the end of the road, and we both knew it. Leticia was still unclear as to what was going on. Before getting into the car, Orlando hugged me, crying, and said, "I am so sorry!" He repeated it several times. All I could do was to hug him harder. We all got into the car, which felt like a sauna due to the island heat. I do not even recall if we turned on the air conditioning because as soon as we got into the car, I started wailing. Orlando joined me with the same sentiment. The sadness was so profound. I had never felt this overwhelming sense of hopelessness. I would come to feel this sorrow again in December 2014 when my beautiful, wonderful father, David, tragically lost his life in a car accident, leaving my dear mom, Forita, widowed after 47 years of marriage.

Seemingly out of nowhere, Orlando and I heard a voice that said, "Jiny, like I told you before, you can borrow my uterus." It was Leticia speaking. I had forgotten she was with us. After hearing that, Orlando and I looked at each other, and cried even more inconsolably. I turned around at some point and grabbed Leticia's hand. In a broken, crying voice I said, "Thank you, I know, but I am not the issue now." Previously, Leticia had offered her uterus to us after the second IVF failed. Right after my words, Leticia instantly saddened, and she too began crying. As a mother, Leticia understood our longing to be parents, and she had been there as we went through the different methods of trying to conceive.

There had been so many failed attempts using the rhythm method, IVF, ovulation method, acupuncture, and tantric sexual positions. We had even filled out adoption papers, but the process was so arduous. In the car that day, though, I finally told Orlando that I couldn't do this anymore. No more trying, hoping, desiring to be a mother. I had no more energy in me. Do you know what it is like every month wishing that your period wouldn't come? We did not plan things too far ahead in case we got pregnant. There were happy moments, but also lonely moments during this process.

I felt like an anomaly because I am Latina and I should be having babies. During this process, we also had a couple of miscarriages. Those pregnancies only lasted a few weeks, but left their mark on me emotionally. Orlando and I felt the bliss of being pregnant both times, and I am thankful to God to have at least let me know what pregnancy feels like. The joy I felt at the thought of being a mother radiated from my very being. We could not share with others, though, because society tells you to wait three months before announcing. Maybe we should have told the world so that the universe knew we wanted this child.

A HEALING PATH

Navigating through a miscarriage is lonely. One moment it is real, and then it is gone. How does one grieve a miscarriage? How do you tell people, "Hey, someone I never knew, never met, did not share with you, and LOVED with all my being is gone?" Part of my frustration was that I did not want to hear folks telling me, "It was not your time," or "It's better it happened now." We chose not to share during these times with anyone, but I did choose to name them even though I did not know the gender. I had names picked out: Marcelino Orlando Miranda and Miranda Onolia Miranda. Marcelino comes from my grandfather on my father's side.

I experienced many firsts with Abuelo Lin. I learned how to smoke a cigar and how to burn beans. Abuelo Lin still brings a smile to my heart. Onolia was my husband's mother, a sweet and loving woman. Even with her last years plagued with Alzheimer's, you could see the love she had for her son, my husband, Orlando. My husband and I were entrepreneurial partners for more than ten years when the recession hit in 2008. We restructured the business so we could operate from anywhere. Nevertheless, my heart at times yearned to be around children. Hence, I decided to become a substitute teacher in our local school district in March 2010. I still was able to run my side of the business. If there were times I could not respond to a client, Orlando could hold them off until I returned from subbing. I began subbing one to two days a week. It was my way to give back to my community, and it also fed my soul. Mind you I was paid, but money was not my motivation; it was and still is being around the children. This has been an exciting venture for me! I would tell others that I do this for fun, but really I did it for my heart!

Substituting provided a healing of my broken heart after our final attempt in Puerto Rico. These past seven years of teaching have been gratifying. It has made me a stronger and more loving person. The fact that I get a chance to teach children, and in turn, they teach me, is amazing. Also, Orlando and I decided to host students from aboard. These past several years we hosted three teenagers. It was a great experience because I had to schedule my activities around theirs, drive them around, entertain them, and cook daily just like parents must do every day. This warmed my heart.

FAMILY BLESSINGS

I am the oldest of three girls; nine and twelve years separate me from Marilynn and Gisenia, respectively. While growing up, I helped my parents take care of my sisters. I was the babysitter during all the days off from school. When they were young, I taught them their ABCs, math, and English. Now that we are older, one of the greatest things about having siblings is their children!

When my sister Marilynn had her first child, Sofia, in 2007, she asked my husband and me to be the godparents, making the birth of Sofia even more special for us. My husband and I were able to experience many firsts with our Sofia, such as going to musicals, concerts, etc. But the most touching "first" was when our Sofia went to kindergarten.

Orlando and I met my sister, her husband, and Sofia on the first day of school. We were there to see her go into the school for the first time. When we returned to our car, this incredible sentiment stirred up inside me, and I started crying. Orlando's emotions got the best of him too. The tears were a result of all of the desires we had for our own children coming to fruition with our godchild. Words cannot describe how blessed we felt to experience Sofia's first day of school. I believe we organically felt what most parents feel when their child goes to school for the first time. After our tears had stopped flowing, we both looked at each other and started giggling. We knew what we had just experienced!

I went from believing that I would never have the opportunity to experience such milestones with a child to actually having those experiences, just in a different way. I am grateful that my sisters have given me the gift of being an aunt. Thanks to my sister Marilynn, I have Sofia (10), Annalys (7), and Antonio (5). My sister Gisenia has Jonas (2). I would do anything for my nieces and nephews. I hurt when they hurt, and I am happy when they are happy. This has taught me that even though I am not a "parent," I can still feel in my heart.

A DESTINATION IS GUARANTEED

What has this journey taught me? Well, first that I needed to forgive and love myself. I used to run through scenarios of what I could have done differently. For example, should I have worked less, exercised more, eaten healthier, prayed more? The list goes on. Ultimately, I mourned that I will not be a mother. However, I rejoice that my life is filled with children, or "childfull," because of my nieces and nephews, children of my friends and extended family, and all the students I have encountered while subbing. I found a way to be a mother. I have learned that being maternal comes from the heart and soul.

My desire for others is that they not judge a childless couple. You have no idea what is behind that door. There are days I have to find the motivation to get up and get going and give meaning to my day. I have come across folks that say, "You should have ..." Well, it is easy to say, but after you have walked in my shoes you can say whatever you want.

Psalm 127: 3-5 speaks of children being a blessing from God. I believe God will not withhold my blessings for not having children. Rather, this scripture is a reminder that EVERY child is to be looked at as a blessing, and not as a burden. Every child that crosses my path will always be blessed, even if he/she is not mine!

My husband Orlando has been my rock. I could not have

taken this journey of conceiving with anyone else, and without this journey, I would not be the person I am today. I love this person I have become. ¡Teamo, Pupi! No Regrets! Lastly, I love you forever Sofia, Annalys, Antonio, Jonas, and those still to come!

REFLECTION

1. What defines you as a woman?

2. What is your self-worth tied to?

3. When the thing you want most doesn't happen, do you give up? Or do you transform your desires to fill your void?

BIOGRAPHY

Jeanette V. Miranda has simultaneously owned and managed businesses ranging from a children's boutique shop to a digital advertising display screen company to a marketing company. Jeanette has been co-owner of Miranda Hispanic Marketing (MHM) for the past 18 years and serves as the Multicultural Marketing Director. MHM is a fully integrated marketing, public relations, and promotional company committed to the U.S. Hispanic multi-national markets. Jeanette has worked with an array of clients such as Anheuser-Busch, Miller Brewing Company, and Novamex-Jarritos, to name a few.

Jeanette sits on the Board of Directors for Latino Treatment Center. She also serves as a coach with the INCubator program at Dundee-Crown High School in Carpentersville, Illinois. As if she isn't busy enough, she also serves as a substitute teacher for the second largest school district in Illinois, School District U-46 in Elgin. Jeanette is an amateur photographer, speaks conversational Italian, and is learning how to play the acoustic guitar.

In May of 2016, Jeanette earned a Masters of Arts in Organizational Leadership from Judson University. Her applied research thesis titled *E-commerce Marketing Services to the Growing U.S. Hispanics Market: Issues and Implications that Come with Major Population Change*, was published.

Jeanette V. Miranda
jeanette.v.miranda@gmail.com
(773) 865-3459

Karina Garden Jimenez

"Stop seeking perfection and approval. You are enough."

Let's start at the very beginning. My parents, one-year-old sister and I immigrated to Long Island, New York when I was eight years old. Although we were comfortable in the Dominican Republic, my parents were looking to provide a better life and a stronger education for me and my sister.

Like most immigrants, my parents faced many obstacles. In spite of them, they started to build a life around their core values and priorities.

What effect did all of this have on me? As the only individual that initially spoke English, I quickly became my family's "American representative." It was a tremendous responsibility, so I had to grow up very quickly. The downside? I didn't have much of a childhood. However, I learned from a young age that only a "can do" attitude was going to allow our family, and ultimately myself, to thrive. This was an invaluable life lesson.

SACRIFICE AND THE STRENGTH TO SUCCEED

Fast forward to my parent's divorce in my early teens. The heavy load continued, as I was forced to become my mother's counterpart in our home. At the time, I felt incredibly needed and valued, since now my mother was unable to tackle all of the responsibilities of being both mom and dad. She was working full-time, while running a household by herself, and she looked to me for support. This newfound responsibility gave me a greater sense of personal accountability and boosted my self-worth; I literally felt invincible. I had a better understanding of how important my contribution was and I took pleasure in playing an active part in our family's progress.

The totality of these experiences created a need to honor all of my parent's sacrifices by leading a life that made them proud, one that realized their "American Dream." So I started down my path early, in elementary school, already pursuing a career that I knew would make them happy – law – and creating a life centered on meeting that one singular goal. Knowing that we were unable to afford college tuition, I excelled at every level of my education, landing a full scholarship to Boston University where I ultimately received dual degrees - a BA in political science and a BS in psychology.

After graduation, I did what was expected of me, and came back to New York to live with my mother and sister. Continuing my carefully laid out plans of achieving greatness, I accepted a paralegal position at a prestigious law firm in New York. So what if I became a slave to the system, absorbed with rising above all of my colleagues and working 12-hour days? I believed in my heart of hearts that only if I went above and beyond and did more than what was expected of me– even if it killed me – would I get a stellar recommendation that would facilitate my acceptance into a good law school.

So after three years of torture, I went off to Brooklyn Law School. I worked full-time to pay for the expensive housing in Brooklyn Heights, took out massive amounts of loans to pay for tuition, became active in student groups, volunteered for local and minority bar associations…nothing was going to stand in the way of wowing a law firm into hiring me after graduation.

I was still carrying responsibility for my family's well-being, while pushing myself for years to near exhaustion from college, working as a paralegal, surviving law school and planning my wedding while studying for the New York and New Jersey bar exams. All of it proved toxic for my emotional and mental stability. Unfortunately, it took many years for me to recognize this.

CONFRONTING MY INNER GREMLIN

I'd checked all the boxes. I had a solid education. I pursued the sought-after career. I settled down and got married. And yet, these accomplishments did not fulfill me. I was still waking up some days wondering, "Is this all there is? Is this it?" I kept asking myself, "Why am I so unhappy?"

I was that girl who was so consumed about how I came across to others that I completely lost my sense of self. On the outside, I was legit. I had a cushy job, a killer husband, and personality for days. But on the inside? I was dying a slow death. I was so driven by advancing my legal career and reaching perfection that I hadn't realized I had collapsed my entire sense of self... my total self-worth was directly tied to my accomplishments.

After a very melodramatic, quarter-life breakdown, I had a total epiphany. I was so over being my own worst enemy. I realized that I really couldn't go on like this. I couldn't continue to make everyone and everything else more important than me. I couldn't keep defining my entire self-worth by my career, and I sure-as-heck had to start being nicer to myself.

Always striving. Setting goals. Checking off boxes. Getting things done. On to the next thing. And like most people, I developed an acute focus on the things I hadn't done yet - the things I hadn't achieved yet. So, while fully understanding that I needed to stop this destructive cycle, I kept pushing. I kept checking boxes. I kept chasing.

And, there is absolutely nothing wrong with pursuit... with achievement or goal-setting. That isn't the problem. The problem was that I kept pushing, and pushing, and pushing, and totally forgot to celebrate my successes and milestones. I lost presence and completely forgot to enjoy the journey.

And so I set out to reprogram my mindset.

When you hear stories about what your parents went through to make it in this country, to forge their own way despite so many obstacles, you realize how privileged you are.

To choose what school you want to go to, to choose a career – these are luxury choices, and I didn't want to squander any of those opportunities, but I also didn't want to continue being unhappy. I started to believe that I was going to live a life that made my parents proud – even if doing so meant that I had to follow my own path, maybe a path that they wouldn't initially understand. It was also important for me to be a positive reflection of a Dominican woman in a culture inundated with Latino stereotypes. And because of these stereotypes, I struggled to believe that I'd be able to go much farther. And so for me, it became about proving myself wrong.

But I couldn't really do any of that if I wasn't living a full, authentic, and happy life. How could I make my family proud and inspire other Latinas if I was leading an unhappy life?

That's when the shift happened. I knew I had to take action and start somewhere, so I focused on removing toxicity from my life. First, I had to confront my inner "gremlin." I had to learn how to stop being so mean to myself. I started to actively identify and switch up internal conversations so that I would say empowering affirmations to myself, instead of all the negative self-talk.

I focused on convincing myself that I was enough by separating my goals from my self-worth. And of course, this is easier said than done. It is a constant battle to fight that small piece of me that is terrified of changing my life's plan, that worries of failing, and that is attached to the feeling that I'm "not enough."

Once I started valuing myself, other changes began to take place. I started to analyze my relationships and decide which I would tolerate.

I read somewhere that when you are on the journey of life chasing big dreams, there is zero space for people with toxic energy. Embracing this and having a no-tolerance policy for negative people enabled me to make guilt-free decisions and gracefully step away from those relationships. I started to surround myself with like-minded, positive people. These friendships are in no way directly advantageous, but they are friends who genuinely understand and authentically support me.

I'm a work in progress to this day, but I am proud of the mindful choices I'm making, and the strides I've made towards achieving balance in my life.

For everyone that has felt or is feeling like I did, I have three pieces of advice.

1. There is no goal that you could ever achieve that will convince you that you are enough. **If you don't already believe it before you get to the goal, you still won't believe it once you achieve the goal.**

2. You are an incredible person. I don't even know you, but I can say undoubtedly that there is something in you that sets you apart. You need to find what it is and embrace it. Nurture it.

3. Other people's opinions, external comparisons, and your own inner "gremlin" may make you question your self-worth. Some days are worse than others, but on every day, realize you are enough.

FUELING MY SOUL WITH PASSION

I had a growing dissatisfaction with my legal career and a fervor began forming. I wanted to pursue my passion. I felt empowered by the rush of turning my business ideas into something tangible and profitable with my natural, "I can do this" attitude propelling me forward.

Recognizing that I wasn't ready to quit law altogether, I pursued a passion for entrepreneurship. I knew next to nothing about starting and running a business, so I educated myself on successful business practices through courses, books, masterminds, workshops, and conferences. By prioritizing learning and furthering my knowledge, I was able to confidently step into my power and start sharing my ideas with the world.

And so my first business venture was born, bluGarden Events, a full-service event company providing concept design, planning and production services. Under that brand, I created the *NY Bridal and Quince Expo* (NYBQE), the tri-state area's first bridal and quinceañera trade show, open to all, but with a particular focus on the Latino community. My goal was to create an upbeat environment where brides and quinceañeras met talented professionals, eager to help them create celebrations that blend current trends with their cultural traditions. I also wanted it to serve as a vehicle to support the growth of local, minority-owned small businesses by providing a new marketplace to promote their products and services. And I succeeded.

It was at the 2016 *NYBQE* that I met and connected with a woman that encouraged me to pivot from a total focus on bluGarden to a greater mission and vision. I had always known that I wanted to dedicate my efforts specifically to empowering Latina women and minority entrepreneurs as they sought to make their mark in the business world, and now I had an opportunity to do that.

For many women, there are simply not enough role models, community or professional networks and mentors available to help guide them through entrepreneurship, especially in underserved communities. Realizing this, I decided to co-found *The Business of WE*. My partner and I wanted to help women entrepreneurs acquire the tools and education they needed to unlock their full potential. Committed to both personal and professional growth, we dreamt of providing a platform for purpose-driven women, a sacred community where they could advance in their entrepreneurial pursuits by providing essential strategies and resources, fostering collaborative connections, inspiration, and empowerment.

The possibility of achieving this vision colored my thoughts, actions, and choices, prompting me to pursue it with an unflappable and joyful determination. I admit that it's a challenge every day to find a balance between my legal career, entrepreneurial drive, and wellness. Sometimes I fail at it, but those setbacks do not trump the excitement and exhilaration I feel as I get closer to achieving this goal.

I finally found my purpose, which brings me closer to living a full, authentic, and happy life. I wake up filled with gratitude because I'm crafting my own adventure.

REFLECTION

1. Have you ever been given more responsibility than you thought you could handle? How did you react?

2. Do you have an unfulfilled passion?

3. Do you feel that you are enough? If not, what steps can you take to change your perception of self?

BIOGRAPHY

Karina Garden Jimenez is a practicing transactional attorney and entrepreneur who has dedicated her career to empowering Latina women and minority entrepreneurs as they seek to make their mark in the business world.

Passionate about entrepreneurship, she is especially adept with the process of business formation and the management of startup contracts. Often serving as a "department of one", her roles have never fit neatly into a single job description. Karina enjoys all things creative, including visual branding, website design, and graphic work, as well as event planning.

Currently, Karina is involved in a number of passion-fueled projects. She serves as a founding partner of The Business of WE, an invaluable resource for purpose-driven female entrepreneurs. She is also the owner of bluGarden Events, a full-service event production company and creator of the *NY Bridal & Quince Expo*, the tri-state area's first bridal and quinceañera trade show.

She's been featured on NBC Visiones, Univision, Telemundo, NY1 Noticias, NPR Latino and 1010Wins, among other media outlets. Karina holds a BA in political science and a BS in psychology from Boston University, along with a JD from Brooklyn Law School.

Karina holds a BA in political science and a BS in psychology from Boston University, along with a JD from Brooklyn Law School.

Karina Garden Jimenez
connect@karinagarden.com
(917) 945-6967

Zory Martínez Jaen

*"When I decided I did not want to keep living my present life,
everything changed."*

Very early on a cold, sunny morning in November of 2007, I
boarded a bus from Xalapa, Veracruz bound for the international
airport in Mexico City. My flight to Chicago was leaving that
same afternoon.

The main reason I was going to Chicago was to accompany
my sister during a very difficult time. To be specific, she was
suffering from a broken heart with severe depression. I had my
own reasons; I wanted to make a change in my life and take a
deep breath. I had no job, and honestly, I was tired of my life
style: working most of the time, earning next to nothing, no close
family, bad romantic relationships, and loneliness. All of these
reasons led me to the decision to take a plane and be with my
sister for a few weeks. I'm glad I did it.

THE LIFE INVENTORY

All five hours on the way to Mexico City, I was thinking
about my mistakes, experiences, family, and decisions. I was not

happy. Then I heard that little voice inside asking, "Why aren't you happy? You are healthy. Your family is not close, but they love you. Love is going to come at the right time." I started to analyze myself and came to the conclusion that for 29 years I was playing the role of "victim." Yes, I finally realized in that bus, that being the victim, or at least acting like one, was a pattern that I had gotten used to. I believe that we unconsciously repeat patterns of our parent's behavior.

Unfortunately, we don't think or even notice when we repeat those patterns in our own character. That morning, I became conscious of why my behavior was affecting me in a negative way, making me unhappy.

One more time, I found myself right in front of this huge wall of doubts and insecurity, with hundreds of questions, and still alone. The reason I mentioned "one more time" is because when I was 15 years old, my parents got divorced. Suddenly, my three sisters and I were living with an awful feeling of uncertainty. While we were going through this, my sisters and I were separated. I even had to leave school for a while. I felt furious. Why would they do that to us? On the other hand, I felt relieved that I would no longer have to witness their fights, which were becoming steadily worse.

Since then, I have developed an ability to make myself feel bad. I used to wonder why I didn't have a united family. Why couldn't my parents fix their problems in a different way? Why didn't they support us in continuing school? I filled myself with many complaints at a young age.

As I took this inventory of my life, I realized that attending a Catholic school for my first few years actually sustained me, and gave me hope. I believe there is something greater, always accompanying me, which guides me on difficult days. My father gave me that. With his effort, I had 11 years of excellent academic education in a private school, which sowed confidence within me as well as an invisible thread of religious faith. That saved me from depression and from falling into some vice with no way out.

I used to say, "To be reborn from the ashes, first you should live in the fire from hell." As a young adult, I had already created my own hell. I built it with the human need for approval: first from my parents, then friends, relationships, etc. I tried desperately to please others, which led to the self-destruction of my own essence and pretending to be someone else. When I realized that these people did not care about my efforts to please them, I became frustrated, disappointed and depressed. The fire of my private hell fed on those feelings.

There were so many days that I came home to my beloved pet Scooby, and the feeling of loneliness was suffocating. I would fall asleep crying, feeling betrayed by life. I was watching how people close to me were advancing in their professional and personal lives while I was wasting my time in the station called "life is unfair." I was there, watching the train pass by.

That November morning, I felt I had to make a change. I was overwhelmed, just thinking, and I did not know how to start. One thing was clear to me-- I was at the end of my tether. I had to stop being unhappy, I had to stop being the victim and be responsible for my good and bad decisions. And why not? I needed to enjoy them and most importantly, learn from them.

I've heard that any day is a good day for a new beginning. That day I started to change my life. On the plane, I started writing a list of what my ideal life would be like. The list was as follows:

1. I won't spend another second complaining about things that I cannot change.

2. I will put myself in other people's places to see their perspective about problems, decisions, or solutions.

3. I will continue giving my best in all I do.

4. I deserve a better job than the one I left behind.

5. I deserve a person, a partner to be with to share my life. I won't say "a prince", but somebody close, simply because I deserve it and I am a good person.

6. I will enjoy every situation in life, good or bad.

7. I will be loving and patient to help my sister.

THREE BIG CHALLENGES

With my list as ammunition, I could now tackle the life challenges I was facing.

My first challenge was a "scar operation." As expected, my sister Lizy was suffering from her broken relationship. In less than six months, she went from a size 12 to size 0. She did not talk to anyone, including me. Her only reason to continue were her two adorable dogs, Piwie and Camila. I gave her space, letting her be. After two weeks, the situation was completely intolerable for me. How can you live in an apartment with someone and just have monologues for conversation? No way. So one night, I confronted her. I made her angry on purpose, to force her to vent to me. It was a very long, long, night but she changed her attitude, positively.

Eventually, she opened the door to the huge amount of possibilities that life offers. She learned how to forgive her ex, but most importantly, she learned how to forgive herself. We repaired her broken heart and she smiled again.

My second challenge had to do with someone trying to humiliate me. After one month in Chicago, I took a job as a coat checker at the restaurant where my sister used to work. It was a very elegant, trendy place. I worked only four hours a day, but I was impressed when I ended up earning more than three days' salary in Mexico.

A week later, one of the hosts began to make derogatory comments about me because I was Mexican. I couldn't believe it. She would say I did not speak English well. She started looking at me with superiority and there were even times when she pushed me in the halls and threw menus at me. She was jealous because I did not have a formal salary, but earned more than her, just through tips. After a while of her relentlessly trying to make me feel bad, I couldn't stand it anymore. I felt powerless because I did not have the linguistic ability to defend myself, so I quit the job.

That night, when Lizy came back from work, she told me that she had put the woman in her place and reported the bullying to the manager. That did not make me feel better, but it was good that Lizy confronted her. As I said before, I didn't want to complain anymore, or feel like a victim.

Instead, I took action. I started an intensive program of professional English at the Universidad Autonoma de México (UNAM), Chicago campus. I walked to and from school from our apartment to save money. I spent half the day at school. The classes were hard. Taking the English course made me more confident and I met very nice people from Mexico and from here as well. They were a big help to me. Meanwhile, the woman from the restaurant who did not like Latinos was fired a week after I quit.

My third challenge was to remain proud of my Mexican heart. In the spring of 2008, I was so anxious. In Mexico, I used to work ten hours a day. I had been here for almost three months and I was not working. I had the need to make money. I thought it was time to look for a job, although after what happened in the restaurant, my self-esteem was still low. However, I would not allow those thoughts to stop me and I stayed positive.

One of the teachers at UNAM told me about a part-time job opportunity for a nanny that spoke Spanish. It was the perfect job for me. I had practice taking care of my three younger sisters and I would not have to deal with misunderstandings because of the language. I made an appointment. The day of the interview came, and I was very nervous.

The address was in one of those big buildings downtown, which made me even more nervous. I pushed the cloud of negativity out of my head, took a deep breath, and knocked on the door. To my surprise, the person who gave me a warm welcome was a six-year-old girl. "Hola," she said in a carefree and friendly voice. I loved it and my stress melted away with that lively greeting.

The little girl and her mother were both interviewing me. The mother was a very pretty lady, warm, and educated. They were Bulgarian. I spent about two hours there, feeling very relaxed and talking about my country. She did not tell me that day if I got the job, but I certainly had a good time. When I finally got word I was hired, they told me they liked the pride with which I told them about my country and the Mexican songs I sang for them over tea and cookies. Until this day, they are my second family.

LOVE AND CHANGE

Life is wise. When I felt hopeless, unloved, alone, I was damaging my essence. I never learned how to love myself. In that condition, you cannot give love or expect it from outside. That's why I always felt disappointed.

When I decided I did not want to keep living my present life, everything changed. I allowed my heart to guide me. At the beginning of my story I did not have a job, a boyfriend, a plan or even any hope. In these three challenges, I let life take its course. I gave up control and resisted my bad habit of complaining and feeling victimized.

I like to think that the deep, strong love for my sister pulled me through my learning journey. My trip was medicine for my inner pain, my second chance to reinvent myself. In this city, my beloved Chicago, I found the love of my life, (remember my wish list...) a good man who is my best friend and shares his life with me. Together, we are living the miracle of our son, Michael Ethan, the most wonderful reminder from heaven that we are perfect just as we are.

Now that America has adopted me, I feel even more proud of my roots. I am Latina, and expressing this without fear has been key to learning to live in a foreign country. Although it has not been easy, it has been worth it.

REFLECTION

1. Have you ever taken the time to make an inventory of your life?

2. Have you ever assumed the attitude of a victim? Did it help you feel better?

3. Have you ever felt uncomfortable being a foreigner?

BIOGRAPHY

Zoraya Martínez Jaen (Zory) was born in Mexico City and is the oldest of four sisters. When she was 16 years old, she moved to Veracruz and began working for the press department in the Government Cultural Institute. She worked there for several years, gaining considerable experience in the area of press and advertising sales. She also served as manager of a branch office in one of Mexico's most important financial newspapers and participated as a TV and radio host.

Chicago became her home in 2007. Today, she is a private Spanish tutor, and teaches Spanish in two Chicago area schools. She is very passionate about the Spanish language. In her words: "The richness in our language is incomparable. We must preserve it and practice it correctly, always with pride."

To spread knowledge of the Spanish language, Zory also tutors writing, orthography and sings Spanish and Mexican songs at cultural and social events. She believes the day that Latinos embrace their roots, they will become more valued and respected as a very important part of the American society.

Zory Martínez Jaen
zor1503@hotmail.com
zorymartinez.com
(773) 930-1736

Leticia Madrigal

"We must come to terms with our health and love ourselves now because tomorrow may be too late."

As a daughter and granddaughter of immigrants and a first-generation American, Dad would tell us to be productive, buy property, and become independent. My father was originally from Nuevo Leon, Mexico and arrived in the U.S. in 1953 to work. He worked in a cemetery for years until he retired and accompanied my mother and oldest sister to the Pilsen community of Chicago, Illinois.

I'm the youngest of my five amazing siblings. I'm told I'm fortunate because my parents were pros by the time I came into the world. My mission is to help humanity. I thank my parents for their dedication to my education and for giving me the honor of being their caregiver. They have truly shaped my life.

MORE THAN JUST DAD

My father, Natalio, was nicknamed "el muñeco" (pretty boy) because he was so handsome. He dedicated his life to moving our family forward while my mother focused on taking care of us. She spent sleepless nights so we'd finish our homework. She was the disciplinarian, "*chiquita pero picosa*," which meant she was little, but she'd bite. Dad was the sweetest, sweet as honey. Reading poetry from the Readers Digest, he'd share his wisdom with me. He supervised my math homework, listened to all my ideas and gave me everything I needed. I loved to tickle him, and he'd squirm and we'd giggle endlessly.

Dad's spirit kept me active at home and on the baseball field. He showed me the beauty of getting in the boxing ring, knocking out adversity and not being afraid to sweat. We walked, biked, and I shared his passion for boxing, baseball, and wrestling. We enjoyed the hustle and bustle of working, going to school, traveling, and enjoying life together as a family.

I was born 13 years after my fourth sibling so by the time I was five years old, my sisters were married and my brothers were out of the house. By default, I reigned as the only child and felt the love from everyone. We have volumes of pictures my dad took over the years. He was quite the photographer!

As I was growing up he'd worry and say, "Don't break anyone's heart, not even boys. Be good, be kind to people." As a child, I was left perplexed. I literally thought I would never break anyone's heart, but I had often broken many glasses of milk. So I thought if breaking hearts was like breaking milk glasses, I was in trouble. I wanted to make him proud. He was a very sensitive and affectionate soul.

After I became an adult I understood that putting him on a pedestal was not only setting him up for failure, it was just not realistic. He was more than a father to me, even more than a role model. He was my best friend. Over the years he made mistakes, and that gave me a chance to make mistakes too, which was okay. Later, I accepted he was perfectly imperfect. I knew he was worthy of many more chances. He taught me to forgive, which is a lesson I am so thankful to have learned.

Dad had a very passive temperament, and was not one to overreact. Instead, he graced us with his suave, calm, and collected nature. He wasn't easily rattled and had a lot of patience for all of us, including my mother.

As a teen, I often clashed with my mom. In retrospect, it was probably because we were so much alike. I'd always take Dad's side when Mom disagreed with him for whatever reason. I was definitely a daddy's girl. When we were fighting, he'd break us apart and say to me, "I've raised you to be good, to be kind, to be the bigger person. Go to school to be educated. Be respectful to your mother." Yikes, when Dad spoke it was as if the earth stopped. He was a man of few words and could literally shift my point of view with just a glance.

ONE DEADLY DAY

One midsummer evening, I got a call from my mother in Mexico. She was screaming and crying. My father had died. I couldn't even imagine my mother being without me or my dad. They had moved to Mexico and had been there for several years. I heard her say the police were there, and that they were waiting on the state police and forensics to arrive. She was being detained for questioning, but she didn't know anything. The whole street corner was blocked off. It was a horrible situation. I remember wishing I could fly and be there for her instantly. I felt helpless being so far away from her.

I caught the first flight to Mexico and learned that August is dangerously hot in my parent's hometown. Dad had suffered a heat stroke, which led to a massive heart attack. It all happened while Mom was heading back to him after being gone for a week for her monthly diabetes and heart lab work. He died and was decomposing. He'd exploded and his bodily fluids were on their bedrooms walls, sheets, floor and everywhere. I saw the forensics team carry him away in a black body bag. We were numb, in shock, and not processing anything. Our hearts were broken.

Fortunately, that fateful day when my mother arrived home, she couldn't find her keys, otherwise she would've died too. She had knocked, called out to him, and banged on the door to no avail. She walked the town thinking she'd bump into him and even waited in the town plaza until late. She told nobody else because she didn't want to bother anyone, and thought he'd eventually come home. She walked back and slept in one of her rocking chairs on the front porch.

The next morning, my aunt visited and immediately noticed the pungent smell, like someone died. She realized my mom was oblivious to what was happening and called the police, who busted down the door. That's when our lives turned upside down.

The day he died, Dad walked to and from the market and returned home about noon on that record-breaking, extremely hot day. I had called him just about the time he left, but I missed him. As he returned from the market, he stepped into a house with no open window, air conditioning, or circulation. It was a steaming sauna and he fell prey to a heat stroke.

Had I known then what I know now about my family health history, my father would still be alive. My grandparents died of heart disease. My father was terrified of doctor visits. He withheld his symptoms from everyone, including his doctors, until his silence led to his untimely death. He thought he was protected from chronic illness due to his love of walking, his commitment to being sober and not smoking, and not drinking alcohol or even coffee. For years he led the local AA groups and helped to create an NA group. His group members came to the funeral to share how Dad touched their lives and the community shared many beautiful stories of their memories of him.

As he approached his 80's, he walked less but he'd eat the same so he gained weight and seemed swollen. He fell a few times, blaming it on his knees. I know now it was his heart. His vision declined. He'd walk with his mouth open and told me he'd stopped laughing "because he couldn't catch his breath." I remember my mom told the doctor that he'd sleep during the day for hours. The doctor told her to bring him in but dad would put it off. Believe me, the signs were all there. We just didn't notice because we were so focused on my mother's health problems.

We failed to see all that my father was going through. He'd often pray that he'd die quickly so he wouldn't be a burden. He needed some extra TLC to get him to the hospital. He was afraid. Sometimes when I think about it my heart is heavy and I could just beat myself up. Then I use a mantra that shifts my state of mind to one of peace. "Let it go, you did enough. You are enough." I breathe and pray for peace in our hearts.

FROM TRAGEDY, TO POWER AND PEACE

Growing up I had an affinity to be of service, volunteering in several organizations. Giving back just felt right. Even though my parents didn't understand what I was getting out of volunteering, they still supported my decisions. Volunteering helped me figure out which direction I wanted to go.

In 1993, Cesar Chavez came to visit in support of the nonprofit National Museum of Mexican Art (NMMA) in Chicago. He said, "Without the support of the community, this wouldn't work." Indeed without the support of our community ¡Amate Ahora! Wouldn't work.

The ¡Amate Ahora! movement creates a culture for leaders and community health leadership. It encourages families to talk about their family's health history and mobilizes communities and the workforce to exercise and be proactive about their health. Today we are present in the U.S. in the Pilsen community in Chicago and in the Dominican Republic in Jarabacoa in the Él Montaña community.

I am incredibly grateful and blessed to have a generous family both here in the U.S. and in the Dominican Republic. I dedicate my education and life's work to my immigrant parents as I stand tall for community health. All thanks to my husband and immediate family and especially Carlos Tortolero, CEO NMMA and his extraordinary team for supporting me year after year and fueling the fire in me and our movement. I couldn't do this work without their leadership and activism. Thanks to all of our fitness participants and instructors, doctors, nurses, agriculturalist, chefs, care givers, advocates, media, collaborative partners, sponsors, resources, organizations, artists, poets, and performers.

¡Ámate Ahora! offers an annual health expo, monthly health challenges, and a fitness program. We also have an adult baseball team for ¡Ámate Ahora! Each player represents a chronic illness and is a voice for health all summer.

We must come to terms with our health and love ourselves now because tomorrow may be too late. We must practice what we preach. We must convert our words into action and break the cycle of chronic disease by knowing our family health history, getting checked and becoming a champion. As a national spokeswoman for WomenHeart, the National Coalition for Women with Heart Disease, I advocate for early detection and proper treatment for all women living with heart disease and also for research funding and policies. I'm proud to be a WomenHeart Champion.

Having my mother and living my life through her eyes is a divine experience. She too has had near-death health scares. When Dad died, my mother had a complete breakdown. She was inconsolable. Emotionally, psychologically and physically, in time we found solidarity with each other. I was grateful that Dad had talked to me about his savings and pension, his insurance and will, and how he wanted things when he and my mom died. He prepared us so we knew what to do and could proceed with grace. As a family we chose to thrive, move forward, and fight her diabetes and heart disease together. After years of living with her unmanaged conditions, her heart and kidneys were compromised. Doctors told her she had six months to live.

Today she's a proud pacemaker recipient and manages her diabetes. I'm a proud caregiver, advocate, and a valvular champion. Yes, I too am championing my heart disease. When it comes to our health, we can never take it for granted. Even if you feel fine, go see a doctor. I can't say I didn't have symptoms because you don't know what you don't know.

Being a caregiver transformed my life. My mother saved my life and Women Heart saved my heart. Get checked. I do. Every year.

REFLECTION

1. Who has made the biggest impact on you in your childhood?

2. How informed are you about your family's health history?

3. Are you doing all you can to manage your health?

BIOGRAPHY

Leticia is the Principal Industrial/Organizational Psychologist at Madrigal Consulting. She creates a culture for community health leadership to come to terms with health issues through education, exploring family health histories, and mobilizing communities to advocate and exercise for health.

She coordinates Ámate Ahora Mañana Puede Ser Muy Tarde, which produces annual health expos in the U.S. and the Dominican Republic. As a TEDx Speaker, Leticia presented From Tragedy to Power & Peace and is the national spokeswoman for WomenHeart, the National Coalition for Women with Heart Disease, representing 43,000 women that live with, are at risk for, or have been recently diagnosed with heart disease. She's fighting her own personal battle with valvular heart disease.

Leticia led a national heart disease campaign in 576 Burlington Stores in 47 States and Puerto Rico, mobilizing 26,000 associates to demonstrate a "Healthy Heart Workforce." She received the 2016 Sor Juan Women of Legacy: Women of Achievement Award from the National Museum of Mexican Art and is also a member of the diversity and inclusion committee for the Chicago Health Executives Forum (CHEF), a chapter of the American College of Healthcare Executives. She is also a premier professional associate for the National Hispanic Medical Association in the Midwest region.

Leticia Madrigal, M.A.
madrigalconsulting@gmail.com
(773) 587.5909

Daisy Jimenez

"Self-awareness is wisdom within."

One of the greatest mysteries in life is how to truly get to know yourself. Part of our human nature is to seek love, acceptance, and transformation. Growing up looking for approval, not being able to say no, and always wanting to do things perfectly, became my learned behavior. I wanted to understand people's way of behaving, but the truth was, I was looking for a life philosophy that was safe and sound.

THE BEAUTY OF SELF-AWARENESS

Self-awareness is the vehicle that helps us to grow physically, mentally, emotionally, and spiritually. Self-observation is defined as watching everything in you and your external world as circumstances that are not happening to you, but for you. There is nothing more delightful than being aware because self-love, self-compassion, and self-esteem will arrive and you will awake to life by being blissfully conscious. Practicing self-awareness, I learned how to experience the pleasure of the senses and how to nourish my mind to fulfill the capacity of enjoyment. No more expectations and illusions; just living in the land of pure love. I discovered that true wisdom was found by turning on the light of awareness.

As a child, I found that creativity was a virtual space where I was protected from the outside world. I wanted to understand myself because I was very sensitive, and could not decode my emotions. I grappled to become less vulnerable. Self-awareness was the first step to mastering emotional intelligence and building a solid foundation to the root of self-love.

There can be challenging moments in life, but observing them helps you find new solutions. As a little girl in Veracruz, I would dream of working in the advertising corporate world. Now, my dream had come true. As time went on, I discovered that I was living in automatic mode, working so many hours, and no longer being fulfilled. So I decided to go to Switzerland, where I learned another type of lifestyle. There, I observed the inner world... where magic happens.

THE HIDDEN BLESSING

Major struggles end up coming from our very own fears, insecurities, and behavior patterns. There are people in our lives that mean the world to us; people who are always willing to give all their love. They are kind, wholehearted, and give comfort when needed. I am blessed to say that my early life was perfectly beautiful, having my grandmother Celia Torres. It was devastating to think of losing grandmother because I found pure love in her. She was my most wonderful gift from God. She nourished my heart with strength and grace, until one day, she passed on.

This event was shocking and overwhelming. I could not understand anything. Where did she go? Where was our relationship? Who was I if she no longer existed? I not only lost her, but I lost my identity, my self-perception.

I cried and cried, feeling sad and blue for months. I had so many questions about what life was all about. Nothing made sense. I could not find any comfort or peace of mind. I cried with all my heart, asking God for help.

The next morning, I was asked if I wanted to become a life coach. I knew deep inside I wanted to discover all the hidden potential within me and do something to invest in myself. I was the first one that could receive help. I needed a new philosophy to grab onto and feel stronger. For one moment, I thought that my grandmother was no longer with me to design my life, but to my surprise, she was still helping me with my transformation, only this time in a different way.

I was aware that I wanted to change, and I was ready for it. Her presence was still very alive and having a big influence on me. It is the thought of separation that makes us suffer. Once again, I returned to the safe place that I created as a child: "creativityland", and I was creating a new virtual place to find self-awareness, which is wisdom within.

THE QUESTIONING PHASE

Curiosity was fundamental during my self-esteem recovery process. I had to disconnect to connect, and question that what was happening in real life is an absolute truth. Once again, who was I? Was I enough? Was I self-compassionate?

How important was the opinion of my family? Was saying "no" going to make me a different person? I learned that being nice was a mission that I had to give to myself first. What is the thin line between virtual self-love and being egotistical? What was the truth? What was my truth? Was a better life waiting for me beyond social beliefs? A different lifestyle? Was I living life with one percent of the possibilities? Were there new ways of creating solutions in life? Where was the source of energy? What does it mean to let go?

As a society, we tend to complain that we don't have time or money, but wanting more time means our social expectations are surpassing reality. Wanting more money means adding more value to ourselves. Learning not to react to external circumstances and having control over our emotions allows us to recognize the real meaning of why something is happening.

Things started to become functional or non-functional instead of right and wrong. I was paying attention to all the voices in my mind to silence them and only listen to the wise self. I was asking if that small idea in my head was a truth or a lie. The source of unconditional love started knocking on the doors of my mind. What was my priority in life? To walk with intention and power? The discovery of a force that burns your heart's desire and makes you move all over the world? Questioning will make awareness connect to your soul's purpose.

THE AWAKENING WHISPER

When you notice all the voices in your head, there is one kind that you truly know is supreme, gentle, and strong. The voice of wisdom emerges from a dark realm to free itself from a disturbed identity. Dive into the ocean of silence and you will go thousands of layers deep into the core of your faith, the place where sensitivity becomes a strong filter to intuition, and authentic self-talk starts whispering in your ear with a rush of excitement all over your body. Then there will be a moment to hold onto, the moment of being good enough. The moment of self-realizing who you are.

Since discovering the voice of my awakened soul, I now have a magic way of seeing life. My beautiful angel Celia gave me the most wonderful gift. I am very blessed to have God, a beautiful family, and friends and mentors that transformed my life, like my son Sebastian Garcia, Fernando Espinosa, Alejandra Llamas, Graciela Torres, Fany Cohen, and Mayra Alvarez. I have become a transmitter of love and am able to help others by listening to their emotions and turning them into creative conversations. I have a new way of living and seeing the pureness of other's souls to create beautiful things with their given talents to serve others.

All the decisions that we continually make are based on love or fear. I choose love.

You will find freedom and growth when you stop protecting your identity. I found out that in order to face challenges, I first had to accept what I couldn't change. Real transformation begins when you embrace problems as a minister for growth. You free yourself when you find yourself.

In between what is true and what we see, there is the perception of our world. Embrace who you really are to create truly authentic, valuable relationships. Accepting the shadows and vulnerabilities will bring light to them. Shadows define the joyful moments. I always say they have a hidden message for us. They just want to be observed like toddlers having a tantrum. It is the first step to heal them. Doubting yourself can be very dangerous because it drains away your power, which allows you to make changes in your life.

The most important relationship you have is with yourself. Respect the quality of your thoughts, observe emotions, read, expand points of view to bring new solutions to life, connect with fully open, wholehearted people and dedicate time to your holistic self. Walk, sleep, hydrate, laugh, cry, play, dance, sing, love, mediate, breathe…whatever you decide to do, just be aware that you are doing it. Life is now. Faith is a decision. Practicing spirituality creates a spectrum of possibilities. When you are in perfect harmony with yourself, amazing people start showing up in your life; people who believe in you, give you opportunity and are eager to share the magic.

The journey continues and still brings so many lessons to learn. However, I live them with peace. Whatever challenges, stress, or anxiety that comes and pays you a visit, having a purpose will keep you on track. Learn to simply let go. Resisting will only make the challenges persist. It is only when we allow ourselves to trust that the path is perfect. Live with the certainty that there will be uncertain moments, but know deep within yourself that a divine wisdom resides that will take each step into your destiny. There are no right or wrong paths. Any of your decisions will take you on a journey where you need to evolve. Live wisely, observing yourself with full grace and acting with great wisdom.

REFLECTION

1. What do you do to create healthy conversations with yourself?

2. What would you create that you wish existed?

3. What is the voice of your true heart's desire?

BIOGRAPHY

Daisy Jimenez is a creative director, photographer, life coach, speaker, and mom. She is founder of Dai Brand, offering branding for small businesses, Organically Creative Photography, and A Delightful Mind coaching. Her mission is to inspire and strengthen entrepreneurs to execute their dreams. She has a segment called *Empieza Por Ti* in the online radio show, *Entre Nosotras*, and has been featured in *Entrepreneur Magazine* and a documentary for NBC Universal.

Daisy has given marketing and self-development seminars at the Women's Business Development Center, the University of Chicago and *Mujeres Latinas en Acción*. She has also collaborated on numerous programs and conferences such as Coach *para Lideres, Tu vida con Proposito* and *Creando Conexiones*. She has worked with national and international brands such as TWI (Switzerland, Dubai & Germany), Kraft Philadelphia Cream Cheese, Broadway in Chicago, Aeromexico Airlines, City of Chicago Tourism, and ComEd.

Daisy received her bachelor's degree in visual communication from the International Academy of Design and Technology (IADT) and was trained as a personal coach at the MAYAKOSHA Institute approved by the International Coaching Foundation (ICF).

She is currently seeking certification as a health coach from the Institute of Integrative Nutrition to help others achieve a healthy lifestyle.

Daisy Jimenez
hello@daibrand.com
(773) 936-7868

Alejandra Chaparro

"Living outside your comfort zone is intellectually stimulating and helps you grow."

Growing up, I was taught to get married to a prince in shining armor, have children, a perfect house, and an enviable job. As a child, I played with irons, Barbies, kitchens, and everything else that emulated household chores. While my female cousins (who I grew up with) combed our dolls' hair, my male cousins created spaceships to make intergalactic trips, but never invited us to go along. My upbringing encouraged me to create a world of comfort without major challenges and difficult things, like as riding on spaceships, building bridges, or anything else considered adventurous. So without realizing it, I grew up looking for things that would provide comfort, because I believed that happiness was in that comfort zone.

OUT OF THE COMFORT ZONE

Yet I always dreamed of traveling the world, knowing many places and people, and having new experiences. I started traveling alone at age nine to visit my father, who lived in Ecuador. My mother worked in a bookstore and brought me beautiful children's books, but I was interested in the others--those which she did not want me to read because they were at a higher reading level and dealt with controversial topics. She locked the bookcase, but I managed to get in and read as many books as I could find. Those books showed me the real world that was not depicted in children's stories. That piqued my curiosity at an early age and developed my creativity and desire to learn many things. Maybe that's where the desire to study social communication was born, a career that would later allow me to discover one part of the world, develop communication skills, and realize that creativity was one of my strengths.

Two years after graduating from Pontifical Xavierian University in Colombia, I married my boyfriend to build the perfect life. At age 24, I already had what I wanted and lived in my comfort zone; I was a professional, worked in *El Tiempo* (the most important newspaper in Colombia), and lived in a wonderful place. What else could I ask for in life? Everything was perfect; so perfect, that I began to get bored. There were no challenges, no dreams, and even at the professional level, I felt that I had already reached where I wanted to go.

A company offered my husband a job in Miami, and we decided to take it. I was not sure what I would do at the professional level there, I only knew it was the opportunity for a change and maybe to have children, but I never imagined it would be a decision that would change my life completely.

In Miami, my husband worked as a show producer for

Discovery Channel. I dedicated myself to being a housewife while studying the language. I went from being a successful professional in Colombia to becoming an economically and emotionally dependent woman in America. Then the problems with my husband began. I was not happy at his side, and he asked me to have children to save our marriage but I did not agree. The gap between us grew larger and the American dream of having a huge house, children, and a perfect life disappeared when my husband lost his job and decided to return to Colombia. I decided to stay in Miami.

We divorced and I did not have a job; it was not my best emotional moment. My family in Miami supported me, but I knew my only option was to take care of myself. The comfort zone I had with him disappeared forever.

I began a new stage in life, and I understood that I had to establish some goals. I decided I wanted to write for all the Spanish-language media in the U.S. So, I started a career as a journalist and dedicated myself to writing articles for various publications on travel, business, politics, culture, food, fashion, and news.

ADVENTURES IN JOURNALISM

One of my first jobs in Miami was with *Agence France-Presse* (AFP). My editor asked me if I could cover a Cuban espionage trial in a federal court and I said yes. My English was not the best at the time, but I accepted the challenge because I had to work. The first time I went to court, the security guards took me out because I had ignored the notices that prohibited tape recorders in the courtroom. It was a criminal offense and I was shocked when I found myself surrounded by security.

The case involved the possible death sentencing of five men accused of spying for the Cuban government, and it was the hottest story in the Hispanic media in South Florida and on the island. At first, it was difficult for me to follow the trial and I wondered why I had accepted such an important responsibility. Then a colleague at *El Nuevo Herald* newspaper helped me understand the complications of what was happening, and I also studied the case in my spare time to understand it.

For several months, I went to the court daily, covered the proceedings in detail and got to know Cuban idiosyncrasy in depth. Years later, Fernando Morais, a renowned Brazilian writer, contacted me to help him gather material for his book "*The Last Soldiers of the Cold War,*" in which he covered all the details and political repercussions of the case. My writing drew the attention of several editors and I began writing for *Travel & Leisure, Poder, El Nuevo Herald,* and other publications. At that time, I was caring for my mother who had Alzheimer's and I could work from home, which was an ideal situation.

After writing screenplays for television shows and articles, I started working on a magazine about celebrities. I interviewed famous singers, artists, and actresses like Sofia Vergara, Juan Gabriel, and Juanes, among others. I covered celebrity weddings, divorces, and even domestic violence cases. My experience in the Miami courts allowed me to find information on the celebrities faster than the competition, so I could write cover stories which sold like hot cakes. I became the journalist who always got the scoop on celebrities, which did not make me very popular with some of them, like Don Omar and Jackie Guerrido.

I was part of the *TVNotas* magazine editorial team that covered their luxurious wedding in Puerto Rico. Unfortunately, the marriage did not last long. After a year, the divorce rumors began. Subsequently, I worked for the magazine's competition, *TVyNovelas* magazine, and I knew that after the couple's separation, only divorce was left. I looked at the Miami courts but found nothing. Someone told me that the divorce suit would be filed in New Jersey. Since everything indicated it was there, I bought a ticket and traveled from Miami to New Jersey. Once in court, I asked about the couple's divorce and they admitted it had taken place. Bingo!

I asked for the divorce records and the two women who worked there practically kicked me out of the office. I waited an hour, came back and asked again but their reaction was more aggressive this time. They closed the door in my face. I had practically lost hope of getting proof, so I called the magazine editor in Miami to tell him that they would not give me the papers and that without them, I could not get the exclusive, or in other words, I would not recover my investment and would end up wasting time and money. I called a lawyer friend and she told me that they had to give them to me because they were public record, so I felt emboldened and returned to knock on the door again, for the fourth time. I told one of the women that the records were public and I had a right to see them. After four hours of insisting, she gave them to me just to see me leave.

I published the divorce exclusive and it appeared on a magazine cover and was distributed in several countries. At that moment, I realized how far I could go as a journalist, but I also decided that it was time to change my career and life. It was time to leave the celebrities alone.

NEW CITY, NEW LESSONS

I had always wanted to move to New York. It was my dream since I moved to Miami, but I was very afraid to live in such a huge city-- so cold, and above all, filled with challenges. I thought about it for several years until I decided to give it a try. By then, I had been in Miami for 12 years, a hot city with beautiful beaches and plenty of space. It was quite the opposite of NYC. If I learned something there, it was to live outside my comfort zone and appreciate the benefits. I discovered that living outside your comfort zone is intellectually stimulating and helps you grow.

Miami no longer offered me the challenge I needed to continue my personal development. I looked for a job that would allow me to move to the Big Apple for another year. The Terra Company hired me to work as a senior lifestyle editor, and that's how I managed to make my way in New York.

At first it was difficult. I did not know many people, nor did I understand how many things worked; it took me time to adapt to the new, cold, cramped city. A few months later, the company began to suffer financial problems. They closed the office in New York, and I lost my job. I remember waking up in a panic in the morning, wondering all the time if I should stay or go back to my comfort zone in Miami. I had received a couple of job offers in Miami, and some even called me crazy because I moved to the Big Apple. At that moment, I had to listen to my heart and follow my intuition to decide what to do.

Losing my job made me think that my financial stability and professional growth should not be in the hands of others or a company. Instead, I was solely responsible for my future, so I decided to take the reins. I had always wanted to be an entrepreneur, to have my own business and not have limits set on my creativity. So far, no work had allowed me to develop my talent and abilities significantly. I understood that only I could do it and that the best way was to create my own company, so I did. I dedicated my first year to creating content for other websites, which was successful. Although I was doing well, I was afraid I did not have enough clients or make enough money. This insecurity prevented me from advancing, but I did not understand it.

After a lot of work on my personal development, educating myself, and relating to the right people, I understood that if I was not 100 percent sure I wanted to be an entrepreneur, I was not going to get the results I was hoping for. My insecurity came not only from my interior, but from my ex-boyfriend, who insisted that it was best to look for a nine- to-five job and forget about pursuing my dream. He himself had tried to become an entrepreneur and had failed.

Overcoming my fears, training myself, surrounding myself with people who believed in me, and using my talent and experience helped me to move to the next level and get invited to give talks and interviews on television. Today, I have clients in several cities whose businesses I have helped grow with communication and social media strategies and whose brands I have helped promote. I feel empowered and able to empower other women like me who have struggled to achieve their dreams. I still have a long way to go, which makes me feel many emotions, but I'm finally on the right path that makes me feel happy and fulfilled.

REFLECTION

1. How many times in the last five years have you stepped outside your comfort zone?

2. What accomplishments make you proud of yourself?

3. What goals do you have for this year and how are you going to carry them out?

BIOGRAPHY

Alejandra Chaparro is an award-winning journalist with more than 12 years of experience in the media industry, including posts in Miami, New York, and Los Angeles. She has directed editorial content strategy and execution for Hispanic publishers such as Univision, Terra Networks, CNN (en Español), and Mamaslatinas.com across a range of lifestyle topics including beauty, food, fashion, and travel. Her areas of expertise include public relations and conducting media training for artists and companies.

Alejandra launched 17 Entertainment Inc. in 2011 to provide social media, content execution, and event planning for the corporate and small business sectors. Some clients include Liberty Mutual, Safeco insurance, Latin-Lingua, LatinaCool.com, El Salvador Consulate and non-profit organizations.

Alejandra was born in Colombia, started her career in Bogota and worked in Quito, Ecuador and Miami, where she worked for a variety of print, broadcast and digital media. Recently, Alejandra was named one of 30 WE NYC (Women Entrepreneurs of New York City) mentors by the NYC Department of Small Business Services (SBS). Her own positive experience with the mentorship program inspired her to give back by joining the 2017 cohort to help women entrepreneurs grow build stronger businesses.

Alejandra currently lives in New York City and loves cooking, working out, and traveling.

Alejandra Chaparro
alejandrac@gmail.com
(305) 761-3560

Liliana Perez

"The worst things in our lives may sometimes turn out to be blessings in disguise."

Life throws curve balls at you. Some you can predict; others come as a surprise. All that matters is how you continue to move ahead despite the unexpected pitch. Many times, these moments happen to us but they aren't significant enough to even remember. However, they all somehow influence who we are today. There are other unforgettable moments that have a greater effect on us than we could ever imagine.

SIGHTS UNSEEN

My curveball came days before I turned 21. I was a student at the Fashion Institute of Technology (FIT) in New York and was on winter break. A normal day included working at my job as a front desk clerk, binge watching TV shows, and doing workout videos at home.

Like many 20 year olds, working out was a big deal for me, especially since I was going to be celebrating the big 2-1. In order to maximize my efforts, I did my home workout videos in a plastic suit to ensure I sweated as much as possible. This was something that I did regularly, and it always felt great to peel off the sweaty suit after the workout.

It was the day following a great workout and everything seemed normal. I had slept well and I felt fine, yet something was going on with my vision. Although I couldn't figure out what it was, I did know that things *didn't look right*. I went to work that afternoon but had to get a ride because I knew that if walking felt strange, driving would be very dangerous. I did my best to get through my shift and I kept my head down whenever possible. I knew I had to see an eye doctor, so the next day I made an appointment with an optometrist who could see me on short notice.

As fate would have it, the doctor I had chosen worked with an ophthalmologist and was able to do more than just a basic eye exam. As he conducted visual test after visual test, I could see the concerned look on his face. I'll never forget staring at two squares projected on the wall and the doctor asking me to tell him when they became one. They never did. The doctor believed that I might have had a stroke and arranged for me to go to New York Eye and Ear Hospital immediately, where they told me I was to have an MRI the next day.

The next morning, after the MRI, I went back home to New Jersey and had barely removed my coat when the phone rang. It was the hospital. The MRI was abnormal, and I was to return to the hospital and be admitted immediately.

I stayed at the hospital for three nights. I received a round of intravenous steroids to correct my double vision, which had been caused by optic neuritis, an inflammation of the optic nerve. I was feeling fine. It was just my vision. It was like a little getaway for me. I got to watch movies on my laptop, read books, and just relax. In typical Latino fashion, despite the hospital rules allowing only two visitors at a time, I had eight visitors in my room at once when my family visited. It was a Dominican party! My roommate also happened to be a very nice Dominican lady who was a pleasure to room with. Everyone said that I looked good and didn't seem sick. I just made jokes about how I would see Tio and Tio's twin next to him.

THE CURVEBALL

On the third day, before I was released, my doctor came to my room to give me my diagnosis. As they had suspected, it was multiple sclerosis. But it wasn't over. Once discharged, I still had to complete two other tests to confirm their findings, including a spinal tap. Then it would be time for treatment.

Everyone was surprised and shocked. No one else in the family had anything like this. Although no one would tell me directly, my insiders would let me know how they tried to trace my life back to the day I was born to try to figure out how this could have happened.

I had just turned 21. I had just been accepted into the exclusive home products development major at FIT and now I had to worry about treating a disease. I'd be lying if I said that I never had moments when I would break down and cry, but despite those moments, I tried my best not to feel sorry for myself. I knew that the release would be good for me, but it ultimately wouldn't do anything.

I decided to educate myself. My goal was to become an expert on MS. I would stare at the MRIs to learn where the abnormalities were. I bought books on the subject that were based on the personal experiences of the authors so I would be prepared when any new symptoms arose. I read about different diets and how countries with Mediterranean diets and those closer to the equator had fewer instances of MS. I was ready to fight. I was a so-called "MS Warrior," or so I thought.

Suddenly, I noticed other symptoms that I hadn't before. There were days that I would be dragging myself on the floor from pain because I was withdrawing from the steroids. But yet, I was still somehow in denial. I didn't care about the symptoms. I refused to miss class. I would be walking by the New York City subway platform and suddenly not be able to feel my legs. I didn't care, and I would somehow keep walking. I was not going to let it take over. However, as much as I refused to let it stop me, I didn't know how else to treat it other than the conventional way that my doctor suggested. I took weekly intramuscular injections that would give me flu-like symptoms. I would take these injections on Friday night and start feeling better by Sunday night, only to go back to school on Monday.

I went to a seminar in New York that was presented by one of the top doctors on MS. The seminar was very informative and I learned more about the medical aspects of the disease. However, there was one thing that stood out to me; I noticed that most of the attendees were women and that many of them were wearing braces or using a cane, a walker, or an electric scooter. It was at that moment when I decided that *I would not be joining them.*

MIND OVER MS

About two years after my diagnosis, I was introduced to a naturopathic doctor. He had a very "different" way of treating patients. He didn't take appointments, and when I arrived at his office I saw that the waiting room was FULL of people patiently waiting their turn. There had to be something special about this guy. At my first meeting with him, I didn't tell him anything about my MS diagnosis. I just sat in the chair and let him take a photo of my pupil. This was strange, very strange. However I was open to it. What he said astounded me. He asked me if I was on a strong medication because he saw that my kidneys were deteriorating. That's all I needed to hear. I made the decision to stop my medication and start enjoying my weekends again.

The naturopath was all about "you are what you eat" so I started to be more cognizant of what I put in my body. I took a lot of supplements and brought a pill box with me everywhere I went. I was feeling good. In the end, I got more than just my weekends back. I was starting to become healthy. It was more than just doing home videos or spending 45 minutes on an elliptical machine. I was feeling good. However, I still wanted to know what was going on in my brain, so I continued having regular MRIs.

The MS was disappearing. I would smile when the doctors

would suggest that I go back on the medication even though there were times were there was no sign of MS on my MRI. It was funny to see the confused looks on their faces.

One of the biggest fears of any doctor who has a patient with MS is what happens to them after they have a baby. It is said that pregnancy is the most peaceful time for an MS patient. All symptoms go away. However, once the baby arrives, symptoms come back with a vengeance.

I was fortunate enough to have a great pregnancy. Once my son was born, my OB asked me to visit my neurologist as soon as possible. I just smiled at him, knowing very well that I wouldn't. My son was born in 2012, and I have yet to visit my neurologist. I'm not sure what my doctor is thinking. Perhaps he believes that I'm one of the lucky ones?

During my current pregnancy, I told him that I practice hot yoga. He asked me if I knew that people with MS shouldn't really be doing hot yoga because of how it raises your core temperature. Raising your core temperature could lead to heat-related symptoms such as optic neuritis (remember the plastic suit?). I did my usual smiling and nodding.

I'm sure many people who are thriving despite their physical ailments have all been told how they "don't look like sick." I have heard that phrase many times and it is usually followed by a request for advice. I'm not a doctor. I'm not an "expert." What I am is someone who has been able to live a life without any physical limitations despite my diagnosis.

I tell them about my diet, my meditation, and how I try

my best to live stress-free, or at least not let things stress me too much. When I tell them about how I've managed to live for so many years without being on medication, they give me a look of skepticism. They assume that I got lucky and many times won't even consider recommending what I did. What they don't understand is that the main thing I did was believe. I believed that despite being diagnosed with a debilitating disease, I would not let it define me.

It has been 14 years since that day in February 2003 when I was diagnosed with a disease that was supposed to debilitate me and reduce my quality of life. It has been 12 years since I had a bad weekend due to my strong medication.

To this day, I still believe that MS was the best thing that ever happened to me. It is my gauge. It is my emotional meter. It reminds me that I'm not respecting my body when I eat poorly and then get tired. It reminds me that I am letting myself get too stressed when I experience exhaustion beyond comprehension. Most of all, it reminds me how strong our minds are when I talk about MS, and I suddenly feel tingling in my knees, after not feeling symptoms for years. That numbness and tingling usually makes me smile, because I then remember that I am a powerful being, and I am in more control than I can ever imagine.

REFLECTION

1. Were you ever able to keep moving ahead despite a major curveball that life threw at you?

2. Have you ever gone against your doctor's advice? What happened?

3. When have you been able to accomplish something that others believed you couldn't?

BIOGRAPHY

Liliana Perez is a first-generation, Dominican-American that was born, raised, and resides in New Jersey. Having learned Spanish at home, she recognized the diversity of Hispanic linguistics at a young age. She wanted to be able to communicate properly with Hispanics from different countries so she took classes for Spanish speakers in high school and in college.

Her background includes hospitality, working as a designer in the home industry, and various roles within the financial industry. She is a graduate of NYC's Fashion Institute of Technology where she majored in interior design and home products. Liliana loves the creative arts and has focused this love into becoming a certified wedding planner. She recently launched her seasonal decorating business, Event Craft Studio, where her products include custom holiday wreaths. Her diverse background helped her obtain her role as the Latino market manager for New York Life Insurance's New Jersey general office.

After being diagnosed with multiple sclerosis in 2003, she has pursued knowledge in alternative methods to heal your body by incorporating yoga, meditation, and emotional freedom technique (aka tapping).

She is the proud mother of Eros (4) and is currently expecting the next addition to her family.

Liliana Perez
lilianarperez@gmail.com
(201) 725-2150

Yanni Sánchez García

"Life constantly teaches you, and if you don't learn, you must repeat the lesson."

I arrived in the U.S. ready to unpack my suitcase full of dreams and ideas. One of the greatest dreams was to be recognized and respected after so many years of studying alongside the best chefs in the world. Boy, did life teach me a lesson!

DREAMS LOST AND FOUND

I remember that summer afternoon of 2009 when I went to Wicker Park in Chicago as usual to supervise the work on *Sabor Saveur*, my restaurant and great dream. I had been working on it for months, and everything had to be as planned. I could touch it, smell it, and see it: the long family tables, dressed in mahogany, with ivory napkins in each place, and the salt-white walls, absolutely refined, with subtle curves that seemed to embrace the place.

I quivered with excitement at the idea of golden-based candelabras with little lights of fire, undulating like poured peach syrup. Did I tell you about the kitchen, that space that has always been a temple for me? There I experienced the meaning of unconditional love, of giving everything without expecting anything in return. There I learned in my childhood the mystique of silence and the voices of the perfect cooking point.

My best friend was with me. We left the premises, commenting on the details of the restaurant, the painting, the chairs, the lights, the atmosphere, everything. The truth is that the visit had been brief, the construction workers had been working very hard, and we were close to finishing. The magical day would finally come when every little corner, salt, pitcher, and utensil would come to life.

Summer days in the U.S. Midwest can be interesting. One day you can melt from the heat under a clear sky, and the next day you may have to hide from the fiercest of storms. The climate is like stiff egg whites: you beat them and beat them and they sponge perfectly, they look beautiful, consistent and give the impression that they are going to stay like this, very stiff and very puffy…and within two minutes they drain out, their pride shrinks and … plop! It's like they're something else.

I had promised the construction workers to stop by the restaurant again and see how the previous day's work had been. And without further ado, I opened the door to discover a hell, which had been extinguished by the morning rain. But in the end, it was hell; everything was lost. My restaurant had burned down during the night. The flames had turned it into an inferno of ashes. The great dream of my life had been reduced to a mound of nothing. I do not know how I managed to keep going. I just took one breath of air, and another, and one more. Then I wiped my tears and took the first step.

GRABBING THE BULL BY THE HORNS

They often say that "you must grab the bull by the horns." I know that for many, this analogy must seem complicated or a bit cruel. However, in this case it fit perfectly!

When I found myself without a restaurant and all the work still ahead of me, I continued forward and moved faster. Even if there was a delay, *Sabor Saveur* had to open. The dream of my restaurant would not be a truncated memory. In the autumn of the same year, after months of hard work, it happened. Opening day of *Sabor Saveur* was one of the happiest days of my life.

The combination of my convictions and my upbringing was good because I go straight for the goal. But on the other hand, there is no halfway point. Well, I must thank my parents. We never wanted for anything and I learned to be independent, value myself, and be responsible for my actions.

I fondly remember those bustling nights when the restaurant was at maximum capacity and we were all concentrated in the kitchen, each doing our own thing, trying hard to make every dish not just a combination of food, but a work of art and tribute to the palate. At the end of the night, we celebrated with gratitude and great respect for the blessing of a new day of work.

After three years of so much work, getting a reputation, name, and loyal clientele, I received a manila envelope that almost ended up in the garbage. You know, it was one of those envelopes with nothing on the outside. But when I opened it, something inside me said, "Yanni, read what comes inside the folder." Thank God I did. It was a folder from the Michelin® tire company with a letter addressed to me, awarding the restaurant a Michelin Star, the highest honor in the industry. The excitement was indescribable. Today I still remember how I barely managed to read those lines because my hands were trembling. And immediately I remembered that fire, the vision of my dream turned to ashes. We had done it; the effort had been worth it.

In 2012, we received the second Michelin Star. And every time, as the award letter suggested, we shared the notification with our customers and celebrated, especially with my team of collaborators, since without them nothing would be possible. Today, with humility, I can say that I am the only female chef with that recognition in Chicago. What more could I ask of this life?

EVERYTHING WAS MISSING

As happens to so many human beings, there came a moment in my life when I felt the need to connect with my own spirituality. A series of readings, intuitions, and personal experiences brought me closer to Buddhism. In 2009, I met my teacher and from that moment I started a process of transformation.

My first lesson was to learn to unlearn, to abandon everything that for me until that day had been vital, and to keep only the essential. It sounds simple and it is, but it is not easy. Especially for a proud and conceited person, whose image mattered, whose ego was great and knew that "nothing had been given to me." I also learned that life constantly teaches you, and if you don't learn, you must repeat the lesson.

When we are in a foreign country, where we must establish new relationships, it is natural to seek your own, your race. To manage my business, I made no exception. For almost four successful years when the restaurant was open, both the accounting and taxes was carried by a compatriot. I, born in Toluca, Mexico, wanted to help my people.

Just as I will never forget that day when the candelabra gleamed and the dishes rang for the first time, I also remember the day the sheriff gave me eight hours to dismantle Sabor Saveur and take out everything I could so it could close indefinitely. Everything ended because of incompetence (perhaps because of my overconfidence), my lack of experience, the bad faith of an individual who never paid my business taxes (and left with his pockets full, leaving my employees with their lives hanging on a thread), and me not knowing what to say, with empty hands and soul.

On July 11, 2013 I had to close the doors of the restaurant, and I was forced to end the greatest dream of my life. That's when you learn that everything comes and goes. What did I have left? Not two dollars in my wallet. I had very difficult times. I, Yanni Sanchez, the chef who had created a restaurant with two Michelin stars, suddenly had nothing to buy sanitary napkins. If it had not been for Alejandro, my brother and my best friend, I do not know what would have happened to me.

Buddhism opens the possibility to understand that nothing happens by chance and if you want to understand your present, you should look at your past. If you want to see your future, you must study your present, because everything has signs and opportunities through which we can grow.

I sought help from countless people, but unfortunately, I soon realized that if there is no money, there is no help. And then appeared Mario Ponce, someone who understands that helping goes beyond yourself. He understands that helping is an act of love, compassion, generosity, and self-abandonment.

EVERYTHING HAS ITS TIME AND MOMENT

After walking from pillar to post looking for opportunities, I got a job interview. However, I had no way to get to that interview since I did not even have ten dollars to put gas into my car. Alejandro, as always, got me out of trouble. When I reached the gas station, I discovered that I had lost ten dollars. I had never felt so unhappy and ill-fated in my whole life, but I forced myself to overcome it. I was worth much more than a simple ten dollar bill, and I was willing to prove it to myself and to the rest of the world. I would show up to that interview. I would be pushing my car or walking on my knees, but I'd be on time. And I left with a prayer over my fear and the little bit of gasoline I had in the tank.

I arrived, the interview was a success, and the rest is history. I was hired as a consultant in September, and after an arduous job,

I opened *Cine* in November of 2014, in Hinsdale, Illinois. The restaurant took its name from the city's great cinema tradition. Little by little, I began to regain my self-esteem. I also discovered that I was no longer the child of the early days of *Sabor Saveur*; now, I was a woman capable of collapsing, standing, and walking again.

But I still had surprises and challenges. In 2015, I met John De Carrier, my mentor, and that same year I was hired as a consultant for a restaurant chain in Pennsylvania. There I grew up, until I decided to end that stage of life and return to Chicago.

And here I've been since October 2016, beginning another chapter and advancing my book, *Sabor*, in which I recount my devotion to love, customs, and my roots, which I will release this year. And while my chef career begins to take shape again, I partnered with two friends and created *Divine Chocolate*, of which there are seven exotic truffles, made with angelic names that many of you have probably already enjoyed.

And the story continues because Yanni is here to stay, thanks to life, my parents, my brothers, Alejandro, my friends and every one of you who can learn something from this story.

Everything happens in its time, neither before nor after. Change happens only when we are ready to receive, when we are full of gratitude, when the ego is something that is not recognized, when we are more human, when we learn to help without expecting anything in return, when money is not purpose but a consequence, and when we decide to be ourselves with all the love that the universe can offer us. Then life continues to teach us and we continue to learn. Just like that.

REFLECTION

1. What signs is your life giving you to make you grow, learn? Are you watching and listening to them? What could you do differently to make your learning less painful?

2. We always talk about "giving without expecting anything in return." When was the last time you did it from the heart, without expecting anything?

3. Yanni says "Idleness is the mother of the best ideas." I invite you to generate ideas about what you can do with what you have at your fingertips. The most difficult moments can generate the best of your life.

BIOGRAPHY

When you have the chance to see Chef Yanni Sánchez García cook, the first thing that surprises you is the pleasure that the onion, butter, and garlic give you; not because they are basic ingredients in the kitchen, but rather because their aroma awakens the senses.

Born in Toluca, Mexico, Yanni has gained vast experience in haute cuisine in prestigious venues such as the Ritz Carlton in Paris and the Mayan Palace, both in Cancun and Acapulco. Yanni completed her training as a chef at the École de Boulangerie et Pâtisserie de Paris.

Her professional training and countless awards, including the prestigious Michelin Award in 2011 and 2012, and ranking as one of *Time Out's* "Top 10 Best Restaurants" in Chicago in 2010, guarantee her talent and passion for soul food.

She is currently in the process of writing her first book, *Sabor*, in which she recounts her devotion to love, customs, and her roots through the kitchen. It is but one of several projects that keep this chef's creativity running high.

She is also the creator of the "Secret Society of Foodies"™ in Chicago, which offers the most exquisite experience of "Dinning with the Chef." ™

Yanni Sánchez García
yanitzins@gmail.com
(773) 996-2552

Imelda (Mely) Shine

"We all need the support and understanding
of our individuality."

I am the daughter of Edna from Mexico and Gabriel from Texas. From the very beginning of my life, everything was blended. I did not ask for that at all, but God had a purpose for me.

BILINGUAL, BICULTURAL MELY

I grew up in Mexico with Spanish as my first language. I do not recall my first English word. I journeyed through the Mexican education system knowing that someday I was going to have my own business.

My entire family is well-educated. I come from generations of entrepreneurs--not just business owners, but entrepreneurs that have passed wealth onto the next generation. So, in college I pursued a degree in business administration and accounting.

As a child, I can remember being surrounded by books, teachers, students, offices, classrooms, copy machines, phones, and anything connected with my family's educational business. Because of this, I knew that my entrepreneurial path was going to be different. I did not want to work in education. I wanted to find a profitable business that did not require the time commitment that my family's business did. My feelings for this are explained in my mother's story in *Today's Inspired Latina Volume I*, which I recommend you read, along with the second volume also! I am proud that my mother, Edna Rodriguez, and I are the first mother/daughter authors of the "Today's Inspired Latina" movement.

In July of 2001, at the age of 18, I became an official adult in Mexico. My mom was planning to move to the U.S., and she convinced me to come "to the land of milk and honey." My plan was to live there for a year to learn English and then return to Mexico to (finally) live an independent life. She, however, was 100 percent sure about moving to the U.S. for good; I saw the determination in her eyes. She sold her businesses and the majority of her properties. I had friends, my own apartment close to the university, and my first official job--everything you would want at that age. Yet, she purchased airline tickets to America for November 22, 2001. I had four months to prepare for a change that would affect everything.

That September, I was exercising and watching TV in the gym when I saw the first crash of the Twin Towers in New York. Everyone in the world was shocked that morning. I thought, "Is that a movie? Is that real? What's going on?" Of course, I figured we were going to cancel our plans to move. However, my mom was still moving forward, and planned for us to be in Chicago as scheduled.

Once I arrived in America, I hated Chicago, the weather,

the culture; everything was a pain. I did not want to be there. I did not like the environment and racism. Also, I did not like my mom at that time. Everything was hard. I did not understand the language or educational system. It was frustrating!

My mom asked some of her friends from Whitehall, Michigan to take me away to learn English and travel with me, since she had enjoyed travelling through the U.S. for business and pleasure. I spent the best four months of my life away from home and Chicago. I would communicate with my hosts using noises and my own sign language, but I returned to my mom knowing more about the language and the culture...a big achievement for an 18 year old!

I thank God for those families that opened their homes to me to teach me about the American culture (the Dickinson and the Peets). They treated me like a member of their family, and my heart will always be thankful.

Once I returned to Chicago, I decided to continue mastering the English language. I knew from experience that people take advantage of you when you don't understand English. It also made it difficult to order food. I remember eating stuff that I did not like because I couldn't clearly order it or explain how I wanted it prepared.

Now I was en route to learning a new language. Every word, every sentence, every paragraph was a challenge but because my perspective changed, everything changed. A few years later, I graduated from the ESL classes. I was working at the same time, so it took longer, but I was determined to make it happen.

Remember the part where I said that I was going to live in the city for a year? Well, that never happened. Instead, I fell in love with the city, the weather, the food, the culture, the people, the school system, and yes, I fell in love with someone else too. I just couldn't say no to this rare opportunity to live in America and become bilingual and bicultural.

The first ten years, I worked in the restaurant industry. I never stopped learning English. I remember being the translator for many situations. I mastered every single position until I couldn't find something new to learn. Then I moved on.

MOTHER AND DAUGHTER DUO

In the summer of 2006, I noticed that my mom wasn't the happy woman I once knew. She was working in the mortgage industry but the light in her eyes was different. I invited her to go out for some mother and daughter coffee time. I clearly remember that honest conversation where I offered my help to make her dream come true. She always wanted to become a motivational speaker for the Latino community. I started being creative, and I just knew that it was the perfect moment.

I launched my first business in 2008, and we named it "*Innovación Vida*" (Life Innovation). As the founder and CEO in conjunction with my mom, Edna, as my business partner, we started the best adventure of our lives. We had our ups and downs (especially downs!) as with any business, but we learned so much. Our mission statement was to be inspired and motivate, educate, and connect the Hispanic community - one person, one family, one community at a time. Our company's motto is "The Best Is Yet To Come "(*Lo Mejor Aún Está Por Verse*).

Keep in mind, at that time, it was a challenge for me because Spanish was not as visible as it is now. People did not embrace the idea of creating something to help the Hispanic community, but we made it happen nonetheless.

It was necessary for Latinos to get motivation, inspiration, education, and connection with others. Today, thanks to *Innovación Vida*, many Latinos have opened businesses, started taking classes, gone back to school, developed better relationships, taken action in their dreams, become public speakers, made great connections with other professionals, started reading more and volunteering, became stronger couples and mended broken relationships, expanded businesses and many other things we probably do not know about!

As a result of that movement, we opened a Spanish book club at the Cicero Public Library: *Innovación*. We know that education and reading is really important for Latinos to move forward. The club is free and open to the community. We meet once a month to discuss motivational/inspirational books. Other clubs opened as our participation grew. The movement continued growing, and Edna launched *Entre Nosotras Radio* On-Line with Esmeralda Medellin back in November 2012.

A few months later, Esmeralda got a job offer in Texas and moved there. My mom was looking for the right partner and asked me to join her. I replied, "Yes, why not? But only temporarily until you get the right person." Obviously, that person is still me.

We have been together, sharing with the community while we carry out our mission: to educate and train women in the various topics that interest them, which includes self-esteem, personal development, family, couples, finance, sex, communication, children, health, cooking, technology, interviews, music and much more.

Currently, Edna is the producer and I am one of four co-hosts of the show and still enjoy it. We are now a well-recognized, international show. I remember when we used to knock on doors asking people to listen or be interviewed on our show. Now, people call us and we add their name to the waiting list!

"Innovacion Vida" has opened many doors for us too. In February 2012, after a phone call which I expected to result in a business partnership, I began a new stage of my life when I was invited to start *Innovación Vida* inside of an interim housing program shelter in Chicago. I accepted without hesitation, never expecting that in the next two years I was going to become the director of programs at two houses for the homeless. I had no experience with homelessness, but I took on the challenge as one sent by God.

If you have ever wondered how it feels to be inside of a blender for two years, that was me, trying to learn and master everything about the current situation of the homeless population in Chicago. After two years, I got a job offer to help an organization with their homelessness prevention contract. Again, without hesitation I said, "Yes, why not?" Today, I am a housing and financial coach, helping families prevent homelessness. It may seem that my career is going backwards from homelessness to homelessness prevention, but actually, it helps my clients see the consequence of not working on their finances.

I believe in Jesus Christ and I just simply know that everything has a reason and a purpose. Nothing in my life happened just because, and I love the fact that my service to the community and to everyone that crosses my path can benefit from the experiences that God has provided for me.

COACHING FOR THE COACH

My work has given me a diverse outlook. We all need love and caring from each other. It doesn't matter where are you coming from, the color of your skin or how much education or money you possess, we all need the support and understanding of our individuality.

Since I function as a coach at my current organization, in March of 2015 they sent me to a 40-hour training where I had a magical moment. One day, we were asked to coach each other in an honest way about a real issue in our lives. I was paired with a female Caucasian coach from a different organization. I shared my situation with her.

"Coach, my issue is that I have spent my whole life in two different countries. I speak English and Spanish and my problem is that I am not from here and I am not from there. Every time I am with Americans, I feel that I do not fit and every time I am with Mexicans, I feel that I do not fit there either. I do not know where I belong."

My partner used the coaching questions that we were practicing, and then in a firm and serious voice she said, "You have something that I do not have; you have powers that I wish I had. Stop saying that you are not from here or from there. You are Mexican AND American; you speak Spanish AND English. The powers that you have enable you to fit in any situation and understand both sides."

At that very magical moment, the wall of uncertainty fell and my whole life changed. I do not know if she realized what she did for me. I just knew I needed to share that message with every person that had the same "powers" as I did, but felt the same way I had for the past 15 years. At one point, I thought, "What a waste of time without knowing the truth," but then I remembered that everything has a reason and a time.

This is my time to share with all Latinas and Latinos. We are powerful and together we are strong. "The Best Is Yet To Come!"

REFLECTION

1. What are three of your greatest strengths or "superpowers?

2. Which action is calling you? What is your mission if you choose to accept it?

3. What EXCITES and INSPIRES you? (Make a list)

BIOGRAPHY

Mely Shine is the Housing and Financial Coach of Center for Changing Lives, a Chicago-based, not-for-profit organization. She possesses many key leadership qualities and is passionate, persistent, direct, a life-long learner, optimistic and creative, hard-working, enthusiastic about building relationships, open to feedback, and energized towards developing people to their fullest potential. She has shown true perseverance and dedication to her work and has a true belief in people and the power of change.

Mely Shine exhibits a commendable and courageous willingness to self-reflect, adapt, negotiate, and try new and different things to build her leadership capacity. She intentionally sets ambitious goals for herself and her teams and has accomplished much in the lives of the clients she serves.

Throughout her work, Mely has remained committed to overseeing and implementing homeless prevention services to reduce emergency situations that lead to homelessness. She deeply believes that we can be the best version of ourselves, and through learning, we can grow and develop our greater purpose and impact. Her own growth as a leader in her community, in her businesses, and at CCL, is the greatest testament to the deep and powerfully transformative truth of that belief. The Best Is Yet To Come!

Imelda (Mely) Shine
imelda.innovacion@gmail.com
(312) 694-5364

Sarah Sanford

"The love I need for myself is where the true power lies."

Rob Liano says it best: "Self-respect, self-worth, and self-love, all begin with self. Stop looking outside of yourself for your value."

THE DIFFERENT ONE

Being Latina, thin, and tall was definitely not usual in my community. At the age of 13, I stood out at 5 feet, 5 inches tall and weighed 85 pounds. I remember identifying with the models in *Seventeen Magazine* because our body images were similar, even though our features, complexion, and hair wasn't. But, that's all I had.

Because I was ridiculed and singled out for my lack of curves and "Latina-ness", growing up in a poor neighborhood in the Bronx, I was never able to see my beauty in the mirror. All I saw was this weird, awkward-looking girl with a big nose, braces, and a long skinny body. But I did have some appreciation for myself. Based on my good friends, I had an awesome personality. I just couldn't figure out how to mesh it all together to feel good and like myself.

I was surrounded by the "morenas" (black girls) who actually made me feel special since they adored my long curly hair. They marveled in braiding and playing with it. However, they never failed to remind me that I was acting "white" or "rich" because I lived in a house, took piano lessons, and studied ballet. I decided to own it and be unique and "punky."

High school was rough. I was very eccentric and threatened for embracing my uniqueness and creativity. Ruffled petticoats with colorful tights, Converse and wild hair, plus being skinny — was a "problem." Everything I did to "be myself" was an issue. As a result, my self-esteem plummeted by the time I was 14.

I remember wearing tights and leggings under my jeans to look "fat" and wearing knit tights under pantyhose to fill out my shape. I became obsessed with weight and fitting in and developed an eating disorder that affected my entire life. I tried diets in reverse, weight training exercise, weight gainers, shakes after meals, and ate everything all the time. I even took cod liver oil injections, which are illegal now. I was able to reach 110 pounds by age 17. I was 5 feet, 7 inches. I felt better and saw progress.

Then came braces after I heard a boy say, "She's cute but when she smiles...yuck!" Yeah, actually I demanded braces after that. I liked the way I looked in them and my smile started to shine and get noticed. Two years later, they came off and it was time for transformation. I began modeling. I felt it was my calling since I was naturally built like a model.

But my self-esteem still wasn't there. I modeled and

competed in the Latin market but was confronted by criticism about my lack of my curves and "Latina-ness." Relying on my new smile and pretty curly hair wasn't enough to get me gigs. I also began dancing professionally in the same market and got the same feedback - great dancer, but "muy flaca" (too thin) - and I still wouldn't get cast.

I started to hate myself and all the women who had that hourglass shape, full breasts, big hips, and curves. Nonetheless, I kept dancing, participating in pageants and modeling, and tried to get into the American market. However, at that time, I was too ethnic and Latinas were not popular unless you could pass for white.

FINDING A NEW WAY

In my late teens, I met a young man who saw my beauty and potential. We fell in love and although we were very young, I married because I believed this would be the only man who would ever see me for who I was and love me even though I was skinny and "not that" beautiful. He encouraged my modeling and dancing. He forced me to wear more sexy clothing and show off what I did have. I did it, just for him.

By my early twenties, I shifted my focus and decided to make a contribution to youth. I started a nonprofit performing arts organization working with girls in my community that I felt had no way to make their dreams a reality. I chose to empower them and via my relationships with them, I saw myself in their eyes. I heard the same struggles with identity, image, and fitting in. I was able to show them how to fight for themselves and push past everyone's opinions and tastes to stand up for who they are. At the same time, I was doing that for myself. I needed to be their example and was no longer able to concern myself with how I looked in fashion shows or dance costumes. In this new role, I saw how I needed to release that thinking and embrace my true self again. I had allowed all that negative feedback to send me into a tailspin to fit a mold, a mold that wasn't made for me. Instead, I needed to create a new mold. I shifted my mindset and boom! I was getting modeling, dance, and video gigs. I felt finally acknowledged and valued by others for my talents and beauty.

Simultaneously, my husband saw the shift and grew more insecure each day as I stepped deeper into my power. He tried to stop my involvement with the nonprofit, performing, and modeling worlds and complained that I no longer focused on "us", although what he really meant was "him." I started to see how I fed off the attention he gave me to fuel my self-esteem. It was ok as long as it never made him feel insecure. Soon enough, we divorced.

THE IMPERFECT PACKAGE

Some years later, I decided to follow my own dreams and enrolled back in school to pursue a career in dance education. I met someone new who I saw as mature, established, smart, financially stable, and overall, the "perfect package." I fell completely in love, ignoring the warning signs. Finally, I was on top of the world. A new career and a new "perfect" guy.

I felt I had what I needed for me to be accepted as successful by my parents and family. He fueled my desires to live a more cultured, classier, upscale life. I was able to build better self- esteem and do things and go places that only classier people did. I felt like it was a real adult relationship. Again, I thought I needed to make it work since I'm really not that attractive. Unfortunately, it all started to quickly fade when I began to experience something familiar, in a much worse way.

I began feeling like I did in my previous marriage. I was built up, then torn down. This time it was accompanied by physical and emotional abuse. I failed to accept that my "perfect" guy was a cocaine addict, alcoholic, and bulimic. Arguments were horrible, and I would physically fight with him because I felt so belittled, so devalued. My relationship became my fear and my dream. My personal belongings were smashed or ripped to pieces and often thrown at me. Anytime I felt good about myself, he would find a terrible thing to say about my hair, outfit, or clothes.

Eventually, I started cutting myself. It started as a suicide attempt but the blood from the surface reminded me that I am real, alive; it calmed me from feeling as if I was the one who was to blame - the one who still couldn't get it right or fit the mold he wanted me to fill. I thought I was a horrible girlfriend and scared he would leave me. I started walking on eggshells and created a "false" self just to keep the peace. I still continued to believe that I had to make this work; that this was the only chance I would have at being with a "real" man. I was now childless in my early thirties.

Finally, I broke. In the midst of one of our routine arguments, I had a severe asthma attack. He thought I was trying to get attention, or even win the argument. I tried to sleep it off but it only got worse. He reluctantly took me to the hospital, only after I begged. He saw I could only speak in a whisper. He still argued. At this point, I checked out and thought I was going to die. I was only able to get a small amount of air in and out.

He finally dropped me off at the hospital at the front entrance. I couldn't walk and he wouldn't get out of the car to help me. Summoning all my energy, I crawled on my hands and knees to the nurse's station, thinking I'd never make it. Finally, someone in the emergency room called out to a nurse to immediately give me an injection for the asthma.

I was in the hospital for three days with no sign of infection, cough, or phlegm. My lungs were clear. I kept sending the doctors back for answers until they asked me, "What's going on at home?" I couldn't understand what they meant, and I still couldn't walk normally around the hospital without getting winded or wheezing. Something was wrong, but I couldn't connect my emotional stress with my asthma.

Meanwhile, my boyfriend was showing up every day with flowers and "acting" loving and gentle. His behavior was so different, I grew suspicious. I knew the moment I got better, I needed to get away from him. I started to see how I was blinded by his demonstrations of "love" after our fights. No longer did I see warmness in his eyes; only pain. It took me two more years and another visit to the hospital (with a torn tendon in my knee due to stress) before I was able to end the relationship.

GRATITUDE AND LOVE

Now in my forties, I found what was missing all those years before: self-love. I was searching for acceptance and validation from external sources: friends, casting agents, my Latino community, my parents and family, and men. Accepting myself was a long journey, but one that I value and appreciate.

First, I never would have thought that those girls I supported and inspired would help me ultimately see all my talents, skills, sexiness, creativity, intelligence, savvy, and versatility. That was more valuable than curves, or fitting in, or ultimately being liked. It allowed me to start accepting myself. Subsequently, the love I needed for myself is where the true power lies. Not in what others think of me, but to validate who I am and give me purpose. They inspired me to hold tight to my dreams, finish school with a master's degree, and become a dance teacher at a performing arts school in NYC.

I'm a proud, tall, thin, curly haired, brown-skinned Latina. I still represent what the culture embodies, curves or not, and I adore who I am. I no longer need anyone's permission to be myself. Now, I can create a life that I love and feel passionate about. I still continue to empower youth and have worked with over 1,000 children. I also have started teaching other women the importance of loving themselves and powerfully moving their lives forward with my program Bold Bella's. I want them to create their own definitions of what being a girl or woman means.

I want them to learn how to redesign their image to reflect the women they want to be, the women that they are meant to be, and the life they are meant to live.

REFLECTION

1. Do you depend on others, including men, to make you feel happy or validated?

2. How often do you say you love yourself in the mirror?

3. What positive attributes about you make you unique and different? How can that be inspiring to others?

BIOGRAPHY

Sarah Sanford is a native Bronx, New Yorker with a passion for education, the arts, and inspiring others to live their dreams. A former NYC certified dance teacher and certified educational leader with a BS from Hunter College and MS from Mercy College, Sarah dedicates her life to mentoring kids of all ages through community programs and public education. She is the founder and director of Siempre Estrellas, Inc. (Always Stars, Inc.), her own nonprofit arts organization focusing on fashion and dance for girls. In schools and the community, Sarah has taught, mentored, and coached children and youth on becoming successful, independent women, especially in the professional dance and entertainment industries.

In 2014, Sarah completed the Momentum Education Leadership program and is now a coach for their adult and teen programs. Her personally designed program, Bold Bellas, empowers women to connect to their feminine power and unleash their inner passions and purpose. She is creating a Teen Bellas program for girls 13-18 and an empowerment program for men. Currently, she's writing her first book, actively hosts and produces arts-focused events throughout NYC with her company Nuvo Arts, and mentors women online.

Sarah Sanford
dance718@live.com
(646) 342-7966

Carmiña Cortes

"Be assured that the universe will eventually guide you to your purpose."

Growing up in a household where almost everyone crossed over to America in the dead of night guaranteed that I was to follow many Mexican traditions. I was first generation Mexican –American, the oldest of three and the first hope of a brighter future for my parents. Consequently, being a starving artist was out of the question and my Apa always said, "Art is your hobby not a job." But art was always present in my life, even as a young child.

My abuelo Enrique sparked that artistic fire. He would make me enlarge the newspaper comic strips as big as legal size paper. At age 14, I was accepted into the Art Instructional School of Minneapolis and received a certificate of completion. At a young age, the universe was already sending me signs. My grand plan since the fourth grade was to become a detective and make my parents proud. Art would just have to wait. The artist Frida Kahlo once said, "At the end of the day, we can endure much more than we think we can." Little did I know I was about to test that theory.

THE FALL

Confusion came over me as I laid on that cold, wet, tile floor of Kentucky Fried Chicken. A sharp pain radiated down my back all the way to my tailbone. It was February 27, 1994. I was a senior in high school, an athlete running track and field, throwing a ten pound shot put around. But what I didn't know was that this fall would change my life forever.

The pain persisted with a vengeance, bringing me to my knees as I screamed for mercy. The instinct of a mother never fails and my Ama's intuition was sending her sirens that something was terribly wrong with her daughter. She drove me to the emergency room for x-rays. All the tests came back inconclusive; we were sent home, baffled. The pain continued for weeks with no answer to what was physically causing the torturous, stabbing pain in my back. Lying in a cold, steel bed in a hospital nightgown brought back memories of laying on that tile floor. The bed moved slowly into this scientific tube and then the ceiling started to cave in. Waiting for the final report of the MRI was like waiting for a death certificate in the mail. The report stated that L4-L5-S1 in the lower lumbar were damaged with a protrusion on L5 which was the culprit of the hideous pain.

A few weeks prior to the fall, I had taken all the required testing to enlist in the Navy. There were two reasons why I become a candidate for the Navy. First, the Naval Criminal Investigative Service enticed me. Secondly, I needed to go as far away as possible to mend a broken heart. After the fall, I was damaged goods and the grand plan came crashing down.

The doctors prescribed medication for the pain as well as for depression, which later would make me co-dependent at the age of 18. I received a series of cortisone shots right into my spine. As the cortisone needle went in, it felt as if someone was scratching a blackboard with sharp nails on my vertebrae. All these procedures consumed me in depression. I recall telling my Apa, "When horses can't run anymore they shoot them, just shoot me now." His response was, "We don't have the money to bury you right now, sorry!" I finally had surgery in November of 1994 with some success.

UPS AND DOWNS

From the fall at KFC, my workmen's compensation paid tuition for a trade school. Not knowing what I wanted from life, I attended American Communications Institute for Spanish broadcasting. I worked for television, radio, and film but didn't find it satisfying. The creative side of the profession did entice me but the environment did not. In 1997, I moved back to the town that saw me take my first steps and where my heart has always been--Santa Monica, California. I signed up for my first semester at Santa Monica College (SMC).

Living on my own proved to be an adventure all by itself. The pain still persisted and the knife stabbing continued on my left side. Walking to school was always a challenge, especially carrying art supplies. Walking up a flight of stairs was, and still is, like climbing Mount Everest without an oxygen tank. Persistence and determination led me to discover who I was eventually meant to be. While there, my passion for the arts grew and I soon realized it was a form of therapy for me. Inadvertently, the universe was preparing me for a world full of creativity.

While in college in 1998, I was hired by the Los Angeles School District as a paraprofessional in the area of special education. Being artistic helped me develop creative curriculum as well as fun art projects. On Valentine's Day of 2002, we handed out goodie bags with candy. The kids were ecstatic and on a sugar rush. As we stood around in the middle of the courtyard, I suddenly felt a child jump on my back. It was a fight of the fittest and I was losing the battle. The child choked me and grabbed on tighter as I tried to swing him off but the child would not release. The other children watched, horrified and screaming for the child to let go. The whole incident seemed an eternity when in reality, it was over in seconds. The pain was horrendous, and I was feeling it all over, from head to toe. The diagnosis for this irreversible injury was three herniated discs in the cervical C1-C2-C3 and L2-L3 in the lower lumbar area. I was prescribed physical therapy and medication once again, along with the loss of my independence and dignity. Moving back into my parent's house destroyed my internal being and a sadness took over my soul. My parents packed up my apartment and my life was put into boxes and pushed into a dark corner of the garage. I was supported financially by my sister Karla and my parents, which destroyed me internally. More than once, I took a handful of my medication, hoping not to wake up.

My week entailed physical therapy, water therapy visits

with psychologists, as well as group therapy. Other days consisted of waking up at 10 a.m., picking up my blanket, walking to the kitchen, picking up a cereal box and ending up on the couch to watch TV until the sun went down. By the end of the day, the cereal box was empty, I was still in my PJs and life was excruciating.

ART AS SALVATION

While digging through a box, I came across my old colored pencils and sketch pad. My brother Rudy needed a logo for his business club at school and so I started drawing again. My sadness brought forth an abundance of paintings expressing hope. Creating brought my dying soul back to life. I even started exhibiting in the Los Angeles area. I shared the views of Frida Kahlo who said, "I paint my own reality. The only thing I know is that I paint because I need to, and I paint whatever passes through my head without any other consideration."

Eventually, the doctor recommended total disability. Devastated and feeling like a failure, I took off to Chicago to spend some time with my boyfriend then, who is now my husband. As he guided me through the Windy City, he walked me over to those famous bronze lions in front of the Art Institute of Chicago. We took a tour of the most prestigious art school in the nation. I felt like a kid in a candy store. In February of 2005, at 30 years old, I applied during portfolio day, where you are notified "on the spot" if you are accepted after a professor reviews your portfolio. I recall my husband telling me, "Don't get upset if you don't get in; it's really hard to get accepted." My response to him was, "I'm getting in!"

The silence while the professor reviewed my portfolio drowned me in agony and I asked my Cuban abuelos to guide me from heaven. He told me the School of the Art Institute of Chicago (SAIC) was expensive and I should be prepared financially. Then, he said that one magical word that made the difference. "Congratulations!" I was accepted and given a merit scholarship along with some private scholarships. The universe had opened the door to the art world and I was running straight through it. It took an injury for me to hear the calling of my passion. The universe had literally kicked my butt in order to redirect me to my purpose.

On a cold winter night, while creating brightly colored wax sculptures alone in the basement of the SAIC Columbus building, a voice whispered, "You're an artist." It was my last year, and sitting there holding the wax, I gave thanks to the universe and declared myself an artist.

2007 was a busy year. I graduated, got married, got a new job and made Illinois my permanent residence. But 2008 was one of the most challenging of all with the diagnosis of my husband's mental illness. It has been one excruciating journey with hospitals, medications, and manic episodes. The lack of information, education and denial of family members exhausted me mentally and physically. This debilitating disorder is like a ripple in a pond; it affects all of us to the core. Having a mentally ill husband is a tremendous challenge. Therefore, more than ever,

I turn to my passion, art.

2009 was the saddest year due to the passing of my mother-in-law, Guillermina, and my Cuban abuela, Amy, but it was the happiest because I held the love of my life, Galilea, in my arms. The day she opened her eyes, keeping my traditions alive and cultivating Latino art became vitally important. Galilea was born with a brush in one hand and a pencil in the other! She was introduced to drawing at nine months and started painting with a brush at twelve months. She brought light back into the darkness of my daily life.

In August of 2014, a friend and I produced an online talk show that promoted all manifestations of the arts. My segment was to introduce visual artists. The show would become the voice of the art world and fill a void needed in the Latino community. It would also fill that emptiness in my soul and act as an antidepressant. It was cheaper than a therapist, and once again, art would safe my life. *Al Ritmo del Arte* is an award-winning show that has brought essential information to the Latino community all over the world. We have been honored to host influential Latino leaders in the art domain. *Al Ritmo del Arte* airs live on Sunday nights via www.aranava.tv.

Be assured that the universe will eventually guide you to your purpose. Don't fight it, but rather, ride the wind. You might fall, but be reassured that there is a reason for it. After a bad situation, something good will come out of it. Ask yourself if there's a message from the universe to guide you back onto your path. Remember that success doesn't come in the form of dollar signs, but rather, how you feel about your journey. Lastly, don't compare your journey to others. You have the exact tools needed to fulfill your purpose and others have what they need. My journey's motto is to inspire before I expire. That's the legacy I want to leave my daughter Galilea-- that her mother inspired another human being.

REFLECTION

1. 1. What are some obstacles that have made you change the direction of your plans?

2. Are you following your passion?

3. Who will you inspire before you expire?

BIOGRAPHY

Carmiña Cortes was born in California and is first generation Mexican-American. At a very young age, her grandfather introduced her to the arts. At age 14, she graduated from the Art Instructional School of Minneapolis. In 2007, she graduated with a merit scholarship from The School of the Art Institute of Chicago with a bachelor's degree in fine arts. She has professionally exhibited her art for more than15 years.

She has more than 16 years of experience in the education field working for Los Angeles Unified School District in special education and for both private and public schools in Chicago.

In 1996, she graduated from the American Communication Institute in broadcasting and communications. Today, she is co-host of the award-winning art talk show, *Al Ritmo del Arte* via www.aranava.tv.

In 2012, she received the MujerDestacada award in the area of culture and arts from the newspaper *La Raza*. She is the recipient of the 2015 Reflecting Excellence award from the newspaper, *Reflejos*. In 2016, she was presented with a certificate of recognition from the City of Pomona, California.

Currently, she serves as program coordinator for the Des Plaines History Museum and loves to explore Chicagoland and its museums with her daughter Galilea #GaliArtz.

Carmiña Cortes
carmina@carminacortes.com
www.carminacortes.com
(224) 565-1805

Itzel Ifatola Luna

"The greatest gift we can give to our soul is to express and fulfill
our true mission on this earth."

When I was in my early twenties, I thought I had found
the love of my life—someone I considered a faithful man, who
wanted to go in the same direction as me. We were in love.
Well, that's what he made me believe, but reality was something
completely different. I had my first daughter, Frida, with him.
She came at the right time. Back then, though, I didn't really
consider it the "right time" to have a baby, but the universe knew
it was.

My daughter came and peeled away many layers that were
built through several years of unconscious living. It's funny how
life works. When you think your life is over because a cycle of life
is coming to an end, you don't think you are going to make it one
more day. Later, you look back and there is that moment when
you say, "*Aha!* That's why that unfolded like this, or that." And
having my daughter Frida was one of those "*Aha*" moments. She
made me more aware of who I truly was, and compelled me to
change aspects of my life for the better.

I really think our children are our greatest spiritual teachers and they bring mindfulness to our crazy adult lives. My little one definitely came and gave me a wake-up call. After deciding to separate from my daughter's father, things became difficult for me. I was mad, sad, disappointed, and tired of myself and the way I was living my life. The only positive thing was my daughter. In that moment, I thought my world was coming to an end, thinking something was wrong with me because although I had my daughter, I was still missing something. During my journey of ups and downs, I got to meet one of the most inspiring and loving humans that I have ever met. He truly shaped me from the inside out.

YOU CAN'T AVOID WHAT'S WRITTEN AS DESTINY

Since my early years, I have always been interested in African culture, but never paid much attention to that feeling. For one reason or another, I always ended up saying that one day I would go to the motherland because something inside me felt a deep appreciation for the Yoruba culture.

I believe that you can't avoid destiny. I am a true believer that what is written with the most high is what unfolds. Do you believe in destiny? Do you believe whatever is happening in your life, it's there for a reason? I do believe that each one of us has our destinies written down and it is no coincidence that we are here. Although many times I have questioned things in my life, I just want to believe that we are here for a reason and we either enjoy it, give a smile and be grateful to life, or we can be complaining and miserable for all our days.

I decided I wanted to connect more with my authentic self-- my spirit-- after attending an event at my college. I met a storyteller from Nigeria that opened a part of my heart that I didn't know existed. He talked to me about his journey through Nigeria, and his many family members in the western part of the African continent. He told me that everyone lived as a big family, but the most important member of this family, was love.

I was listening closely to the wonderful stories he told me. After talking for an hour, he gave me his business card and told me to contact his family members in Nigeria, who were part of one of the largest families in the Yoruba traditional culture. He assured me that they would be able to guide me.

That night, I went home and started searching online. I came across a very gifted and special soul by the name of *Ogunbiyi el caballero de Ifa*. We started talking online for hours at a time and I asked him if he could teach me more about his culture. I told him I had a deep respect and admiration for the Yoruba traditional culture and belief system, from what little I knew about it.

Every night, we had a chance to talk and discuss life in general and sometimes my daughter, Frida, would talk to Ogunbiyi too and tell him about her day at school. I knew he was a very loving friend to Frida and he liked her a lot.

He repeatedly invited me to Nigeria and insisted I go. I honestly felt deep in my heart that I should because I had learned so much already about his culture, but now I really needed to experience it for myself.

A few months later, I spoke to my mom and asked her if she could take care of Frida for me so I could make a trip to Nigeria. I was a little nervous; I didn't really want to go by myself since I didn't know the country, but I didn't wanted to expose my daughter, either.

DESTINY FOUND

The summer came and I was ready to embark on the adventure. Although I had never met Ogunbiyi in person, I felt a deep trust and connection towards him.

The big moment came. I arrived in the western part of Africa, in Nigeria, and I was going to meet that very special person for the first time ever. Although at that moment I didn't know much about him, I still felt like I had known him for a lifetime. We always felt a deep love for each other-- a true connection since day one-- something that is hard to explain with just words.

Not knowing what to expect, I got off the airplane and there he was with his big, almond-shaped eyes and delightful smile. We hugged and smiled at each other. He grabbed my bags and kissed me on the cheek and said, "Welcome, my wife to be!"

I thought that was pretty funny. He had just met me in person and he already wanted me to be his wife? But deep inside my heart, I felt an immediate connection with him. I knew he was a special soul because of the way he talked and expressed himself, with so much love, especially to others.

After driving for a few hours, from the airport to his

hometown called Oshogbo, we finally arrived at his home. As soon as I stepped out of the car I could smell the palm trees and the sweet hibiscus flowers while the drummers played welcoming, praise songs. It was such an amazing experience and right away I knew this was part of my soul; this was what my soul was craving.

That's why I always say that following our intuition is so important. It's our soul communicating, and the greatest gift we can give to our soul is to express and fulfill our true mission on this earth.

While being in Nigeria with Ogunbiyi, we communicated so much on a deeper level, it's hard to explain with words. The connection we had was so profound that only the soul can feel it and if the soul feels it, you reflect it on the outside with love towards yourself and others.

Things were going magnificently and I was learning so much about the Yoruba traditional culture. Ogunbiyi was such a great tutor guide. He took me to a very sacred place in Oshogbo and at that moment, I knew we were meant for each other. He spoke so well about his family, and all of them were so beautiful and eccentric in their own way.

Being in Nigeria for a whole month was an eye-opening experience, and I established a true connection with the man I like to call my soul mate. Ogunbiyi opened my eyes to a whole different dimension here on earth and in the underworld (spirit realm). I saw things within him that I didn't know existed. He told me to always believe in myself, and that our ancestors would help us lead the way, but I had to first connect with my true self, which was my soul.

After leaving Nigeria, we were dating and in love. We had so many plans ahead of us. He loved my daughter, and although he didn't meet her in person, he was always asking if she needed anything. Going back and forth to Nigeria and being able to take in the culture was such a delight for me.

NOTHING ON THIS EARTH IS FOREVER

By then, Ogunbiyi and I got engaged, and soon after, we found out that I was expecting. At first, we were both in shock but still so happy because since day one when I met him, Ogunbiyi had always told me, "You will be the mother to my children." I didn't pay much attention to that but I knew when Ogunbiyi said something, he actually meant it.

Ogunbiyi was a very loyal person. I had never met someone so sincere and loyal before, but at the same time he knew all the right things to say to keep me grounded and to always BELIEVE that anything can happen as long as we are willing to do it and we are still on earth. We were both so excited about our plans and the coming baby that we could barely hold our excitement. We felt so blessed.

He was waiting for his graduation in November so that he could come to meet me in the U.S. When I left Nigeria during the first week of August, we held hands and prayed that everything was going to work out and that the baby would be a fruit of our love. But like everything in life, things can be so unpredictable.

It was a Sunday morning when I got a message from one of his friends asking me if it was true about Ogunbiyi's death. He told me that Ogunbiyi had been in a terrible car accident and didn't survive. I was in shock and could not believe what I had just heard. I was three months pregnant and now I learned about him dying? It just didn't seem possible.

I called his family and they confirmed that he was dead. It was a tragic, horrible nightmare. I collapsed on the floor and started crying and crying. My heart was hurting and my soul was in shock. It was too much to take in. Plus, with my daughter next to me crying, and the baby in my belly, it was a moment I will never forget. All the plans we had for the four of us were just words now because he was never coming back.

After being in shock for days, I finally came to realize he wasn't coming back and that I was never going to see him in this lifetime. But the connection we had was so strong, I know deep in my heart he is always with me in spirit. I believe that where true love exists, there is no separation between the ones in spirit and the ones S.S (Still Standing). Now, he is the one watching over us.....our spiritual guide.

I have had dreams about him, saying he is there with me. "No need to cry, I'm always with you," he says. In another profound dream that I had, I was holding my daughter in my arms and I was crying, when suddenly I saw a light from far away and a woman's voice saying to me, "Why are you crying? There is no need to cry because this baby is Ogunbiyi. He came back in this child. Life continues, don't cry." When I woke up I couldn't believe it, but I felt so much peace inside me, that I knew it was real.

I am a big believer in feminine power towards life. I feel that this was a message from the Holy Mother because where death shows up, life follows. And like my title implies, since you are born gifted, you will never lead an ordinary life. There will always be a sort of laceration that marks your life, but don't worry. This only happens to the strong and brave souls like you and me.

REFLECTION

1. Are you really doing what your soul craves?

2. Are you following your intuition? Do you feel like you are being truly honest with your authentic self?

3. Are you mindful of every moment? Are you thankful for life?

BIOGRAPHY

Itzel Ifatola Luna is learning from her daily experiences. She has become more aware of life and takes one day at a time to be truly mindful of each and every moment.

Itzel lives in Aurora, Illinois and is working on a degree in social work. She wants to be able to help people and to share what she has learned through life. She believes that as older and wiser women, we need to step up and share our stories with the world because there is so much need of healing.

She has learned to be present in life and not take anything for granted. She dreams of one day having her own business and helping people overcome difficulties in life through a more mind, body, and spiritual approach. She loves natural remedies and likes to create sacred time for herself and spend time with her two adorable daughters.

Itzel Ifatola Luna
itzel0508@hotmail.com
(630) 205.8241

Lorena Labastida

"You don't realize you can, until you have to!"

We were fighting again, and I was crying again. Here I was, in America, away from friends and family with a man who had turned from encouraging and supportive to belittling and mentally abusive within the first five years of marriage. Once again, his terrible words had struck through my heart and had reduced me to a crumpling ball on the floor. Then my little daughter Mia, who could barely walk, came over with a tissue. "Mommy don't cry," she said, attempting to wipe my tears. That was the low point. With my child now trying to help me, I knew that I had to take control of my life somehow.

Divorce is never anything we expect. In fact, my whole life was turning out completely unexpected. I was not supposed to be living in Chicagoland, within an unhappy marriage. I was supposed to be happily married to a rich man, raising children and living near my wealthy parents in Mexico, protected and cared for. I was supposed to be living the princess life!

THE PRINCESS LIFE

I was born in Guadalajara into a wealthy family. My father was an entrepreneur and his family had some fame in Mexico. His cousin even ran for president. My mother was loving and supportive.

My three brothers, my sister and I lived in a wonderful house and never wanted for anything. I never had to clean my room, wash my clothes or do chores. We attended excellent, private Catholic schools where we received the finest education. My life was steady, predictable and required very little from me. My parents took us on amazing vacations all over the world and we even had a vacation home in Puerto Vallarta. In the summer, I would stay at the University of Nebraska to learn English.

My dad was proud of his station in life because he had not always been so lucky himself. He made sure we all went to college and I earned a degree in business administration and finance. Then, I expected to go to work for my father, but he surprised me when he refused me. He said that I needed to be independent and work elsewhere. At the time, I didn't like that idea at all, but as I grew older, I appreciated why he did what he did.
So I began my career working for a bank in Mexico. Soon after, a friend introduced me to the man I would marry.

I was dating him when he told me he got a job offer in the U.S. I figured right then and there we were going to break up. After all, I had no interest in living in America! Then he asked me to marry him, and I knew this meant I would be accompanying him to America. Because I was young, in love, and thought life would always be wonderful, I said yes. What I didn't realize was how hard the adjustment was going to be.

ALONE TOGETHER

Before, I had been to America for brief vacations. Now, we arrived with two suitcases, intending to stay forever. We rented an apartment in Elgin and my husband started his job in purchasing. For me, obtaining a work permit was easy since I had already traveled and studied in the U.S. The hard part was being in a foreign country, thousands of miles from my friends, family, and support system. They had all been amazed at my decision and I really didn't know how it was all going to work out. The first stumbling block, however, was to get a job.

That was a very humbling experience. In Mexico, I was climbing the corporate ladder. In America, I was struggling to reach the bottom rung! I took a job as a teller, but soon moved to the bookkeeping department. My husband and I bought a house in Aurora and we had our first son, Javier, in 2003. My mother-in-law, who was now living in the states too, did not want to see me work and told me so. However, I felt it was something I had to do. I returned to work part-time, and soon after, we moved again, this time to a larger home in Yorkville. It was a perfect home for our growing family, but a difficult commute for me. I thought about staying home, but then I heard about a job at a bank in nearby Aurora so I started there in 2005.

A year later, I became pregnant with my second son, Juan Pablo. I was on maternity leave when I got a call from my manager asking if I would consider an assistant manager position. Although I was uncertain, I interviewed and received the offer. I negotiated my full 12-week maternity leave before starting, but I actually returned two weeks earlier than expected. I loved the job. The following year, a branch manager position opened up at my bank and again, I was unsure whether or not I should go for it. My own branch manager, who called himself my "brother from the U.S.", encouraged me to step forward. I did, and got the job! I was the branch manager there from 2007-2014 just before I had my daughter, Mia, in 2013.

Unfortunately, while my career grew stronger, my marriage weakened. The man that I found encouraging and pleasant in Mexico soon turned disgruntled and mentally abusive in America. He continually told me I was worth nothing and that without him, I would be nothing. He was sarcastic and belittling and did everything he could to tear down my self-esteem. Our fighting escalated, and unfortunately, my children were often witnesses.

One day during an exceptionally turbulent time in our marriage, I had to take Mia to the pediatrician because she wasn't feeling well. I remember standing in the office, watching the doctor examine her. For days I had been crying, and was increasingly unhappy with my life and my marriage. I must have looked terrible, but I had pulled myself together long enough to be there for Mia. The pediatrician finished her exam and then, with a sense of authority mixed with compassion, she turned to me and said, "She's sick. But you're sicker." She convinced me to start taking care of myself, and that began with seeing a therapist. My therapist never told me to file for a divorce. But she did help me recognize my dissatisfaction with my life and how destructive it was becoming to my self-worth.

Meanwhile, my husband was also continually dissatisfied with his job and had hopped from one company to the next since we had arrived in America. Now, he had an opportunity with a company in Atlanta. The very idea of moving reminded me of coming to the U.S. and leaving my support system behind to be with only him. I had finally built a new life with friends and workmates in Chicago. I knew I would lose if I followed him again. I did not want to go.

He left to start his job in Atlanta in August of 2014, and we agreed it would be best for me to stay back with the kids for school. Perhaps we both knew that the separation would do us good too. It was a tearful goodbye, especially when he said goodbye to little Mia.

In December, we took the kids to Disney with an incentive that I had earned through work, but we spent much of our time fighting. He liked preferred people in Georgia to those in our hometown, and he was anxious for us to move. I told him that if he would tell me he loved me I would move to Georgia. But he couldn't.

Over spring break, I brought the kids down to Atlanta. We stayed in a rented apartment in a very affluent, upscale Atlanta suburb where he wanted us to live. As I looked around, I realized we would be one of the only Hispanic families there. I also knew he would hardly be home because the job required a lot of travel. It didn't feel comfortable, and I just couldn't warm to the idea of moving again.

THE NEXT CHAPTER

My therapist once told me that life is all about choices. When I returned home, I realized my choices were to uproot the children and once again leave my support system behind for a crumbling marriage, or file for divorce. The very thought scared me. I knew he'd be mad but I also realized I couldn't go on as I was. In April, after returning from the trip, I went to see a divorce attorney in tears. She told me I wasn't ready and to come back. I returned in June, more determined than ever to start proceedings.

I remember how depressed I was the day before I filed. The kids were away at a summer camp in Wisconsin and it just happened to be Father's Day. I knew he was living the life of a bachelor. During his last visit, I had seen his texts to a social group from work and suggestive texts from other women. The courier had a hard time finding my husband to serve him the divorce papers, but they finally caught up to him at work. Then you know what he did? He came home!

He stepped through the door like nothing had happened. Then he took the kids out for ice cream and told them about the divorce himself! That move led to an even greater level of hurt and pain in our family. I asked him to leave the house for good, and I remember standing in the garage watching him leave. His final words to me were, "*El diablo se te aparecio!*" (You have no idea what's coming to you!) I closed the door, and changed the combination to the keypad.

Funny thing was, he was right. I didn't know what was coming to me…which was a surge of strength to carry on alone.

Suddenly, I had strength for my family and myself that I didn't know I had. My cousin, Margarita, who is like a sister to me, says that the Lorena she grew up with did not have this strength. She will tell you I seemed fragile when something happened that was out of my control. She will tell you all I wanted was to grow up, get married, have children, and live near my parents. But now she will tell you how proud she is of my perseverance and how I've faced my fears and insecurities so far away from my family. She didn't realize I could do it…until I did it. And I do believe for most women facing divorce, that is often the case. You don't realize you can, until you have to!

Now I am the sole provider for my children with a new, more visible position as V.P of a well-known bank branch that I have worked hard to expand. I am out in the community connecting with others and representing the bank. My children are thriving in school and participate in activities they want such as football and boy scouts. We live in a townhome and my heart swells whenever I am able to tackle a household project without anyone's help. It's a really good feeling. I have many angels in my life who form my support system. They are there for me when I need them, and even when I don't realize that I do!

For me, I feel validated for making my decision when I see my children succeed, or when they are asked in school to write about their hero and it turns out to be me. If you are in a similar situation, you need to know that you can do it. I didn't think I had the strength, but there it was, hidden deep inside. Perhaps it's there within you too!

REFLECTION

1. Did you ever have to start at the bottom when you felt qualified to be at the top? What did you learn?

2. Has anyone ever "changed" on you? How did you react?

3. Where do you find your strength?

BIOGRAPHY

Lorena Labastida serves as Vice President of Retail Banking and Branch Manager of Aurora Bank & Trust, a Wintrust Community Bank. With over 15 years of experience in retail banking and management, she excels in building relationships as part of her strategy to achieve goals. Lorena delivers superior financial results and best-in-class customer service to create a proactive sales and service environment so her employees can deliver the best possible experience to customers.

Lorena began her banking career in 2001 with Elgin State Bank and has been described by her colleagues as a "driven branch manager, who is always going above and beyond." For the past 12 years, Lorena has enjoyed her proactive involvement with the Aurora community, offering the bank's services to a growing number of businesses and entrepreneurs. She currently sits on the board of the Aurora Hispanic Chamber of Commerce.

Lorena earned her bachelor's degree in business administration and finance from the Universidad Panamericana in Guadalajara, Mexico. However, her proudest achievement is raising her three children, Javier, Juan Pablo, and Mia.

Lorena Labastida
lorlabastida@yahoo.com
(630) 907-0934

Ximena Atristain Bigurra

"Above all, live your life with passion."

I was born in the sixties, in the highest capital city in the world - La Paz, Bolivia - at 12,000 feet above sea level. I am proud to be Bolivian and I love maintaining my traditions and identity in the U.S.

I am a free spirit that lives life with passion. My measure for success is feeling deeply satisfied inside and being emotionally fulfilled, rather than appearing externally successful and being materially fulfilled. I have been married to my husband for almost 27 years and have two girls who are my inspiration and joy in life. I feel I am a very lucky woman to have balanced life as a mom, as an entrepreneur career woman, Bolivian dance teacher, contributor to the community and town commissioner.

Through time I have learned to be very independent and I am fiercely determined to continue on this road no matter how many hard obstacles life puts in my way. I believe life goes on no matter what. If I feel down and stop, the clock will continue ticking minute by minute; it won't wait for me. All I have is to keep moving forward, period. This is the attitude I developed to overcome problems and have a very positive attitude towards my life. It hasn't always being this way. In my teenager years I was very shy and reserved, however I was able to overcome it. Like other people, I have also had many ups and downs through life but it is better to look at it as a beautiful sunny day than a cold, dark and rainy one.

SHAPING MY PERSONALITY

I am the second of my father's five children. Just before I turned two years old, my mother died of an asthma attack at the age of 24. My dad moved my brother and me to his parent's house so my grandparents could raise us. They were so loving and caring.

Grandma, who I called mommy, was a big influence in my life. She always told us the story about being the first woman to wear pants in La Paz and how she wanted to be a lawyer in the 1920's, but her dad said she was crazy. After trying hard to convince him that she wanted a profession, they came to an agreement and she became a teacher. The bottom line is she wanted a career no matter what, which was very advanced thinking for a woman in that time period.

Both of my grandparents went to college, enjoyed reading and taught us the importance of education. We knew that for us, education wasn't an option; it was expected. However, I also inherited my grandma's crafty side and her family's free spirit. Many of my uncles and aunts were theater actors. Having being raised by my grandparents, I think I became more attached to traditions.

Since I lost my mother at a young age and watched my dad remarry a few times, I think I felt it necessary to fill the void of not having a mother. I recall one time when I was seven and going to a birthday party, I saw most of the kids with their parents and I felt so lonely I started crying without even knowing why. I think inadvertently I developed many relationships in which I played a very maternal role, and at the same time I became a leader. For instance, I was very protective of my friends. They called me the mom of the group and I was also the class representative. Later on, when I married, I took a similar role with my husband. Then when I had my two girls, I filled that emptiness, but at the same time they became the center of my life and everything else revolved around them.

DANCING DAYS

Since I was a little girl, I enjoyed putting on make-up and I loved designing dresses and dancing. I used to pretend I was a famous dancer when I visited my maternal grandmother's house, and I used to imagine myself in the theatre, dancing. I wanted to belong to a Spanish dance academy like a lot of girls in school but my grandparents didn't want to register me. I think it was mainly because they didn't want me to become as free-spirited as some of the people in my family. So I participated in school shows and as soon as I graduated from high school, I joined a Bolivian dance troupe called *Ballet Folclórico Municipal De La Paz*. It is amazing how doing what you love can transform you and transport you to a different dimension where you feel and live that moment so intensely.

One of my fondest memories of the troupe is when I had the opportunity to travel with them and represent my city, La Paz, at the "FestiFront" Festival in Yacuiba (Tarija, Bolivia), where singers and dancers from different parts of Bolivia and northern Argentina performed. The first day, we all lined up and sung our Bolivian anthem. That moment is recorded in my memory and will never go away. Even now I feel the goose bumps and emotion I felt for representing my city through the dance.

My love for dancing followed me to the U.S., where my dad and I moved to join my older brother in Chicago in 1984. I arrived at the ripe young age of 20 with so many dreams and expectations for my new life. Even though I thought I knew the language well, I had a hard time understanding all the different accents from the diverse people in Chicago. I remember starting a job at the Sears Service Center and couldn't understand the first sentence my supervisor said in training. It got worse when I had to take care of customers and talk about repairing their lawnmowers and parts using words I had never heard before.

I promised myself I would become economically independent, which I did by working two jobs. I bought myself a car so I could get to work and college.

In Bolivia, I had completed one year of college but in America I decided to start over and study interior design. I kept my passion alive by forming a group of Bolivian folk dancers and filling it with college friends that I recruited. For performances, I would sometimes join forces with another existing dance group in Madison, Wisconsin. Later, a newly formed Bolivian organization called *Renacer Boliviano*, a nonprofit organization that also had a dance troupe, asked me to teach dance classes for children, which I did, and enjoyed immensely for a short period of time. In 1994, I was contacted again to lead the dance troupe for a couple years until I had my second daughter in 1996. Besides Chicago, we traveled to Washington, D.C. and St. Louis to perform.

When my girls grew older, I took them to dance classes in my former Bolivian dance troupe so they could learn the same folk dances I knew. At first they were not that interested, but a few years later, they were really enjoying the troupe and having fun learning about my culture and folk music.

I became a member of *Renacer Boliviano* in 2011 and helped them in different ways. I led the dance troupe for three years where I had the chance to teach my girls. I dedicated a lot of my time and even sewed costumes. I became the president of the organization, and am in my second year of leadership.

I am very proud to be part of *Renacer Boliviano* because we work hard to raise funds for the less fortunate people in Bolivia while also showing our cultural pride through dance. We have performed at the nationally broadcast Mc Donald's Thanksgiving Parade in Chicago as well as many other festivals. We also do three major fundraising events and I have had the privilege of donating our proceeds in person, with my family, to people of Bolivia. These moments were priceless and motivated me to do even more this year to raise funds while celebrating our Bolivian food and culture.

HOW MOTHERHOOD INSPIRED ME

Like I said, becoming a mother was very important to me because I naturally needed to fill that emptiness of not growing up with a mom. Instead of continuing a career as an interior designer, I decided to be an at-home mom when my first daughter was born. I started a home-based business sewing bridesmaid dresses, curtains, kid's outfits, costumes, etc. I had learned to sew by watching my grandma, who made a lot of my dresses and knitted a lot of sweaters. She really never taught me but because I liked it, I learned.

Encouraged by my business, I began studying for a degree in fashion design. I studied part-time a couple days a week while one of my daughters was in preschool and the other was with a babysitter. For four years, I worked at home from dawn to dusk while raising my two daughters. It wasn't easy to work at home, study, and be a mom but I was able to do it for a while.

Eventually, I slowed my business and started working outside the home in my current career, selling skincare and make-up for the past 19 years. This new career gave me the opportunity to dedicate more time to my children at home and help them participate in school events and extracurricular activities. I was in the PTA (parent teacher association) and was a parent representative of my children's classrooms.

Junior high and high school were the times I enjoyed most with them, especially their jazz and contemporary dance competitions outside of school. I organized the teacher appreciation week for two years in a row and helped with costumes and makeup in their activities like theatre, band, and pom-pons. My older daughter always volunteered me for anything that had to be done, like cooking, chaperoning, sewing, organizing, etc. Even when she started college, I helped with her extracurricular activities. I loved it!

Today, besides leading *Renacer Boliviano*, I am slowly getting back into my sewing business and am part of the multicultural awareness commission in my hometown of Hoffman Estates, IL. We are in charge of several events, including the Hispanic Heritage Fiesta, where I organize the entertainment. My mission is to show the community that Latin America doesn't end in Mexico but encompasses a broader spectrum of music, dancing, and costumes which are unique, yet similar at the same time.

PRIORITIES AND BLESSINGS

I can say that being a mom has always been my number one priority. I fully enjoy every single moment of motherhood. I dedicate more than 100 percent to this part of my life and I feel very proud to have kept my husband's Mexican and my Bolivian traditions alive and to have passed them on to my daughters. They are proud Mexican-Bolivian-Americans!

I thank God for letting me be part of my daughter's lives and involved with their activities. I'm also glad that I was simultaneously able to manage my career along with motherhood. With the dance group and all the volunteering I juggle, I am proud and humbled to be starting a new stage in my life as grandma to my youngest daughter's son, who illuminates my being. I hope to pass along my traditions to the next generation.

If I am inspiring to younger generations it is because I am a Latina who lives life to the fullest, or so I'm told! I have a lot of passion for everything I do, I am strong and very confident, I love my age, and I still have a lot to give and to learn. I accept that the road I have traveled has built my character and made me the person that I am. My advice to young Latinas is to be truthful to yourselves, believe in yourself and above all, live your life with passion.

REFLECTION

1. What is your number one priority in life? How do you show it?

2. Do you think you live your life with passion? Why or why not?

3. Is there a way you can give back to the community using your talents and gifts?

BIOGRAPHY

Ximena Atristain-Bigurra, a native of Bolivia, is a leader, entrepreneur, avid performing arts lover, and a Bolivian dance connoisseur. She is the President of Renacer Boliviano, Inc., a nonprofit organization that raises funds to support various causes in Bolivia that help the less fortunate. Ximena has led *Renacer Boliviano* dance troupe from 1994-96 and from 2012-16. Under her leadership, the troupe has captured the heart and spirit of the Bolivian community as well as people in the U.S.

She is also a member of the Cultural Awareness Commission of the village of Hoffman Estates, heading the annual Hispanic Heritage Fiesta. She has a bachelor's degree from Columbia College in interior design and an associate's degree in fashion design from Harper College. Upon graduation, she worked for an architectural firm until her first daughter was born, then launched Designs by Ximena, a fashion and dressmaking business. In recent years, she has been working in the make-up artistry and skin care business and returning to her sewing business. She is married to Aquiles Bigurra from Mexico for the past 26 years and they are the proud parents of two girls and happy grandparents to a baby boy.

Ximena Atristain-Bigurra
xmatristain@gmail.com
(847) 909-8806

Dolores Monterroso

"It doesn't take any more effort to dream big than to dream small."

It was time. I was finally moving forward towards a lifelong dream that would provide security for myself, my husband, Guillermo, and my two daughters.

I searched the business registration forms for the town of Cicero, Illinois to check the box for the business I wanted to register, but "coffee shop" wasn't there—only "restaurant." That wasn't right. My dream was to open a very special coffee shop, unlike any other, that would bring the community together to love and support each other. Who knew years later, my dream would become my reality!

REFLECTIONS OF ADVERSITY

At that point, Guillermo and I had been through a lot. Although Chicago was our home base, we lived in California for several years to be near my oldest daughter, Sejal. We were there when she had her two sons, and when she got a divorce. Years later we moved to Texas, closer to our relatives in Mexico. From move to move, we battled many challenges, especially with Guillermo's health.

Twenty-five years ago, Guillermo was diagnosed with diabetes. However, eight years ago, he began to show severe symptoms of neuropathy, which affects his circulation with devastating effects. He has lost vision in one eye and has only 15 percent left in the other. He also suffered a stroke, and has difficulty walking. Most recently, he began dialysis and is in need of a kidney donor.

Luckily, I was raised with a positive attitude towards adversity, thanks to my mother. My mother lost my father when I was nine years old, back in my little port village in Guatemala. She never remarried and kept his love alive with stories. With my two older sisters, Gloria and Rebeca, I learned from an early age that hard work and perseverance will get you through the tough times. Both my mother and father also taught us to be entrepreneurs. They would say, "It doesn't take any more effort to dream big than to dream small."

I remember waking up, milking the cows, going to market and selling our dairy products before I headed to school. They believed in the importance of education and encouraged us to use our imagination to envision what we wanted, and how to achieve it. Most importantly, they taught us not to focus on our suffering, believe everything is happening for a good reason, and look for love everywhere. They showed us that love and security comes with connecting with others. How right they were!

DISCOVERING COMMUNITY

One of my first jobs in America was as a bilingual secretary for two kind-hearted, wonderful doctors from Rush Presbyterian Hospital in Chicago: Dr. Steven K. Rothschild and Dr. Lisa Salinas. When Dr. Rothschild wanted to open a clinic in the Hispanic community, he asked if I would be his translator. It was a wonderful opportunity to serve others. We opened the clinic in Chicago's Pilsen neighborhood and I began using all the people skills I learned from my mother. I built relationships in the community, and the clinic grew. Then the doctors needed a business manager and Dr. Salinas encouraged me to take the job. I did so under the condition they would continue interviewing for a more qualified person. But I was determined not to disappoint them! I worked hard, learning new medical terminology, and taking courses. I got the job, but soon noticed the cost for the outside billing service was beginning to climb. I told the doctors we could do it in-house for less. Once again, Dr. Salinas encouraged me to take on responsibility and once again, I told them to keep interviewing because I felt underqualified. A few months later, I got that job too!

Since the clinic was so successful, I helped open new ones and streamline the billing in their other locations. Eventually, I even opened my own practice, M & L, which I ran for six years, providing billing support for physicians.

I loved my work, but most of all I loved the opportunity to serve a community. At that time, Dr. Rothschild was visiting many geriatric patients and I would do home visits to them too, offering companionship or whatever they needed. Another doctor opened a clinic for the homeless, and when the director of the shelter transferred elsewhere, I stepped in and truly enjoyed the job.

I spent some of my happiest days working for those doctors. Sejal and her younger sister, Veronica, were little then, and would often come to work with me. I remember the holiday parties for the shelter residents with the girls in attendance and Guillermo playing Santa. The doctors were endlessly supportive and those years truly shaped me as a professional and community giver. I will always be thankful to them for showing me the meaning of community.

PULLING TOGETHER

When Guillermo and I moved to Texas, his diabetes was under control with insulin and he got his HVAC license. He was enjoying his work, when he had an accident that led to a loss of sensitivity in his hands and rotator cuff surgery. He was in severe pain, taking medication, and was no longer working. Unfortunately, we were not only struggling with health issues, but also crushing business complications in Illinois.

A few years prior, we had purchased a commercial building in Cicero and Guillermo had operated a deli and store there. Later, we rented it, but when the tenants left, the building fell into disrepair and quite rapidly, we accumulated thousands of dollars in back taxes. Twice we had buyers interested in the building and both times they fell through. The third time, we were basically giving it away and the buyer said he would pay the taxes. But deep inside, I really wanted to somehow, some way, keep the building for my daughters. And it was about that time, with our financial pressures at their highest, and Guillermo facing increasing physical challenges, when we got the news about Sejal.

Guillermo and I were in California visiting her and the boys when she walked in the door with Veronica. Sejal looked tired. It was then we learned she had been receiving treatment for cancer for months and had just returned from a round of chemotherapy. Veronica knew all along and had been traveling back and forth to support her.

"Why didn't you tell us?" we cried, and she told us we had enough to worry about and she didn't want to give the cancer any more energy and attention. "I don't want you to waste a second of your life feeling pity for me. What I want is for you guys to get back on track again," Sejal said.

Veronica agreed. "Mom, it's really affecting us the way you guys aren't settled."

Their words hit me like a ton of bricks. They were right. We were stuck, mired in health and business problems, not knowing what our next move should be. I couldn't believe Sejal was worried about US. But I knew I had to do something BIG to bring peace to my daughter. I immediately began praying for guidance.

That visit, the three of us spent time together, cherishing the present and refusing to fear the future. The girls made me recall that years ago I had told them that after I stopped working, I wanted to own a café.

"I can't now," I replied to Sejal. "Not with Guillermo so sick.

And I want to take care of you."

"You will help me more if you are independent," said Sejal. "Start putting your business plan together!"

Maybe this was the message from God? If this was the big thing I could do to bring my daughters peace, this is what I needed to do. After all, I had the building. But I still had one major obstacle...money.

As we were leaving, Sejal told us she had a gift for us. Then she handed us an envelope with a check in it and told me it was for the café. Veronica did the same. My eyes filled with tears and I held them close. This was going to happen. For them.

THE MIRACLE OF COMMUNITY

An inspector friend told me that even though the town of Cicero didn't have a box to check for "coffee shop" on the business registration form, they would probably approve us if we created something that would "wow" them.

So we took a chance and began creating my vision....a Christian coffee shop that would function as a meeting place for the community to hold worthwhile events. I even had the name ready...REVIVE, a named formed from the first letters in five important words that resonate with the journey of my family:

Resurrection
Empowerment
Vitality
Inspiration
Vision
Excellence

The words begin with the same first letters in both English and Spanish.

I taped newspaper over the windows, hired some contractors and began remodeling the space to fulfill my vision. My inspector friend said we were only legally allowed to do cosmetic changes to the building, so we had to work without permits or even utilities from the city. We used generators to power the equipment and lights that we needed to work. The project was slow going and took about two years since I did it as I had the money available.

Meanwhile, Sejal underwent several rounds of chemotherapy and was now trying natural, alternative medicines, including nutritional supplements. This inspired me to hire a chef for the café and specialize in healing foods as well as traditional favorites. I worked with him to develop healthy, unique menu items, while catering events to help support the construction project.

April 23, 2014 was my grandson's birthday, the opening day of *REVIVE*, and the day of the big miracle. Sejal called me and told me that the doctors said the cancer was gone. She refused to use the word "remission." Instead she said, "I'm healed. I feel in my heart that I'm healed. God doesn't cure halfway." Our entire family breathed a sigh of relief.

Meanwhile, we had indeed "wowed" the city. They did penalize me for what I had done, but also expressed their gratitude for bringing such a new, unique twist on the traditional coffee shop concept to the city of Cicero. *REVIVE* is based on Christian values and offers a daily menu of made-to-order,

Italian-inspired items prepared by an onsite chef. The café offers corporate catering, and welcomes art, entertainment, comedy, poetry, spirituality, and meetings of business, church and community groups. It offers an upscale atmosphere with linen table cloths, designer furniture and Colombian coffee that customers prefer over Starbucks. Live, instrumental music provides a peaceful atmosphere and we also bring the community together for cultural dinner/theater-type events where we pair the tastes of a certain culture with their native entertainment. This coming summer, we will open an attractive, wrought iron-fenced, patio seating area. I have also started holding monthly events for Latinas, aimed at empowering them, and helping them reach their dreams.

Slowly, we began building a vibrant community that regularly gathered at *REVIVE*. Guillermo spent time there and made many friends too. It reminded me of the communities I had built while working for the doctors at Rush, and it gave the café a sense of belonging and purpose.

We didn't realize how loving and giving this community was, however, until we found out how desperately Guillermo needed a kidney transplant. Because of his other health problems, he did not have enough time to be put on a waitlist. So, we held an event at *REVIVE* and found three donors interested in helping him!

Who knew starting a café would produce such a beautiful, supportive community. They are our extended family and we feel blessed for all that we have been given. From an initial dream, to where we are today, dreaming big brought us to a community of love!

REFLECTION

1. Do you dream big or small? What would it take for you to dream big?

2. How do you define community? How do you build it?

3. What communities do you belong to? What do you learn from them?

BIOGRAPHY

Dolores Monterroso is the owner of *REVIVE*, a Christian-based café located in Cicero, Illinois outside of Chicago. The one-of-a-kind establishment features made-to-order, Italian-inspired items prepared by an onsite chef, corporate catering, live arts and music performances and meeting space and special events for churches and businesses.

After enduring many financial and physical hardships within the lives of her family members, Dolores named her café *REVIVE* as an acronym spelled from the first letters of five words that relate to her Christian faith and the journey of her family: resurrection, empowerment, vitality, inspiration, vision and excellence. The café is located at 5612 W 35th St in Cicero, Illinois.

Dolores has a long history in community building, having served for 22 years as an administrator with Rush Presbyterian Hospital and their satellite neighborhood clinics. She is also the former director of Pilsen Homeless Services.

Originally from Guatemala, Dolores has spent most of her life in the Chicagoland area although she has lived in California and Texas too. She holds a real estate license in Texas.

Dolores has been married to Guillermo, her dedicated husband, for almost forty years and has two grown daughters and two grandsons.

Dolores Monterroso
dolores.monterroso0@gmail.com
(630) 723-4986

Jackie Camacho-Ruíz

ENTREPRENEUR, AUTHOR, SPEAKER, PHILANTHROPIST, TODAY'S INSPIRED LATINA FOUNDER.

Jacqueline Camacho-Ruíz is an award-winning entrepreneur, international speaker, philanthropist and author of nine+ books, including The Little Book of Business Secrets that work published in 2010. She is the founder of The Fig Factor Foundation focused on unleashing the amazing in young Latinas. Jacqueline is a regular guest on local and national TV, radio and print publications.

She has received many prestigious awards, including "Influential Women in Business Award," "Entrepreneurial Excellence" Award and "Annual Awards for Business Excellence" by Daily Herald Business Ledger, "Best Under 40" by Suburban Life, "Unsung Hero" by the City of Aurora and "Woman of Distinction" by Kane County Magazine. As a two-time cancer survivor, Jacqueline possesses wisdom about life well beyond her years. She lives in the Midwest with her husband and business partner, Juan Pablo Ruíz, and her two children. In her spare time, Jackie enjoys flying airplanes, racing cars and experiencing the beauty of life.

For more information, visit www.jackiecamacho.com.